SEVENTY SCOTTISH SONGS

Selected and arranged by

Helen Hopekirk

DOVER PUBLICATIONS, INC., NEW YORK

Published in Canada by General Publishing Company, Ltd., 30 Lesmill Road, Don Mills, Toronto, Ontario.

Published in the United Kingdom by Constable and Company, Ltd., 3 The Lanchesters, 162–164 Fulham Palace Road, London W6 9ER.

This Dover edition, first published in 1992, is an unabridged republication of the edition originally published by Oliver Ditson Co., Boston, in 1905. The frontispiece and epigraph have been omitted, and a publisher's note and a glossary have been added.

Manufactured in the United States of America
Dover Publications, Inc., 31 East 2nd Street, Mineola, N.Y. 11501

Library of Congress Cataloging-in-Publication Data

Seventy Scottish songs / selected and arranged by Helen Hopekirk.
1 score.
Folk songs, arr. for high voice and piano.
Reprint. Originally published: Boston : O. Ditson Co., 1905 (The Musicians library)
ISBN 0-486-27029-7
1. Folk songs, English—Scotland. 2. Folk music—Scotland. 3. Songs (High voice) with piano. I. Hopekirk, Helen. II. Title: Scottish songs. 70 Scottish songs.
M1746.S5 1992 91–759988
CIP
M

CONTENTS

CONTENTS

PUBLISHER'S NOTE

HELEN HOPEKIRK'S Scottish collection first appeared in 1905, one of several national anthologies in the extensive Musicians Library series published by the Boston firm of Oliver Ditson.

Hopekirk was herself a song composer, but was better known as one of the foremost Scottish pianists of her time. Born in Edinburgh in 1856, she studied with the legendary Theodor Leschetizky, made her debut with the Leipzig Gewandhaus Orchestra and concertized on two continents. Though she eventually settled with her husband in Massachusetts, where she died in 1945, her great love for Scotland revealed itself in her many original settings of the national poetry of Fiona MacLeod (William Sharp) and in the care with which she prepared this, her only anthology.

The arrangements are full and sonorous, often calling on the harmonic resources of mature romanticism, and traditional voice leading strongly influences the lines. In the style of the art song—and of folk-song settings of a century earlier—the piano part does not include the melody and most of the settings comprise little introductions and codas. Since most of these tunes were originally conceived as pure melody without any chordal accompaniment, they often subtly resist classical harmonization; they frequently end on notes other than the tonic, employ scales of less than seven notes, and seem to vacillate between relative major and minor or between harmonies on the tonic and the lowered seventh. Nonetheless, arrangers steeped in the Scottish tradition have contrived excellent accompaniments, of which this collection contains more than its share.

The persistence of only a few not obviously superior songs in the Scottish folk-song repertory outside Scotland is noted by Hopekirk at the beginning of her introduction, and despite her efforts and those of other conscientious anthologists, her observation has dated very little. Such beautiful songs from this volume as "I'm Wearin' Awa', Jean," "I Climb the Mountains" and even "Turn Ye to Me" are still largely unknown in America. And more recent anthologies that might rectify the situation can hardly be found in the New World today.

The wealth of Scottish folk song is so impressive that even in this generous selection there was no room for "Ca' the Yowes," "Bonnie Dundee," "Scotland the Brave" and a handful of other well-known songs. But Hopekirk, in keeping with her own conception of her mission, proves herself a connoisseur of the lesser-known. It is hoped that this volume may rekindle interest in the neglected national repertory that it so abundantly represents.

SCOTTISH FOLK-SONGS

OF the Scottish folk-songs here gathered together, I feel it is unnecessary, even were it possible, to enter into a detailed history. The origin of many has been long since lost sight of, owing to their having been orally bequeathed from one family or generation to another, and also to the confusion of races in the country. But as there is some misconception of the nature of Scottish folk-song, belonging as it does to two racially different peoples, the Celtic Scot and the Lowland Scot, a word or two about the general characteristics of both races and their ways of living may help to a better appreciation of their songs, the most beautiful of which are the least known. To many, mention of Scottish music merely recalls to mind a few melodies such as *Auld Lang Syne*, *Blue Bells of Scotland*, *Annie Laurie*, etc. They, and such as they, are only a small part, and not the most beautiful or significant by any means.

Lowland Scottish music and Celtic music, although talked of collectively, are widely different in character. The Lowlander is placid, pastoral, canny, pawkily humorous, somewhat matter of fact, good-hearted, reserved. The Celt is imaginative, "dreaming dreams and seeing visions," unpractical, superstitious, tender, of quick perception, living an inner life, a good lover, a good hater. The Lowlander would die for a dogma, the Celt would die for a dream. The origin of many of their melodies has been lost sight of, some of the so-called Lowland ones having been brought over from Ireland by the settlers about Galloway, and others from England. They are easily discernible by any one who has the scent; for those who have not, it does not much matter. In spite of the beauty of many of the real Lowland melodies, which are principally of an idyllic and pastoral character, it cannot be denied that the Gaelic music far exceeds it in interest and in emotional, weird quality. The old melodies of the Gael have little affinity with the modern major and minor modes, and that makes them seem strange to those who have been nurtured on these scales. What seems bizarre and curious in them to some people becomes perfectly clear when referred to the ancient modes. In many arrangements the melodies have been altered, lowered sevenths raised, etc., to make them smooth for "cultivated ears," thereby taking the very life out of them. Apropos of this, a curious incident happened some years ago. Some one rearranged the Gaelic church service hymns, raising the sevenths, to make them more "modern." But when it came to practice, the discord, that resulted between the few who could sing the raised seventh and the many who could not, made them quickly return to the old way.

The use of the "snap" is also a characteristic of many of the Scottish songs, but is not so prevalent as believed, although largely used by composers who wish to write in Scottish style. A melody written on the pentatonic scale, introducing one or two snaps, is not quite enough to produce the requisite atmosphere, as is proven by the banal melody of *Within a mile o' Edinburgh Town*, written in the eighteenth century by an Englishman, James Hook. There are more sad than gay melodies in the Celtic music of Scotland. "The brain of the Gael hears a music sadder than any music there is," says Fiona MacLeod. When a lady in Edinburgh played *Lochaber no more* to Robert Burns, he cried out, with tears in his eyes, "That 's a fine song for a broken heart." This could be said of many of the old Celtic songs, whether of France, Ireland, or Scotland. The Celts delight in songs of unhappy love, parting, death, the might-have-been; and their melodies are full of the sadness and beauty of the long, tender, melancholy northern twilight.

The manner of singing of the Scottish Gaelic people is also something strange. They stand or sit very quietly, with an utter absence of self-consciousness, and the tones come out rather monotonously; but as the song goes on, one is strangely moved by a subtle something—a wild irregularity of rhythm, something ancient, remote, more easily felt than expressed. The quaint Gaelic language, the old-world melodies, the quiet and pathos of the way of singing, are haunting. In their festive gatherings, the company make a sort of circle, reaching their plaids or handkerchiefs to each other; and as they sing they sway their bodies from side to side, gently waving their plaids about to the rhythm of the song. There are also queer little grace notes introduced between the notes of the melody. As a child I remember hearing a beautiful old Highland lady over eighty years of age sing Jacobite songs to her own accompaniment on an old spinet-like piano, with such a little, sweet, pathetic voice, and with so many of these little grace notes, that it has ever since been one of the outstanding memories of my childhood. My maternal grandmother also had that quaint way of singing, and it used to be *the* pleasure of the church service to me to hear "Granny's graces" added to the decorous performances of the others.

Two influences have been powerful in stifling that impulse towards expression in music which has been for years the inheritance of both Gael and Lowlander. The first was the introduction of a hard, merciless Calvinism at the time of the Reformation. The aim of that seemed to be, not to "glorify God and enjoy Him" and His gifts of the beautiful "forever," but to glorify Him by despising these gifts as a sacred duty. Scotland is only now recovering from that blight. Another influence was the Anglicizing of everything Scottish since the Union—"girdling the world with Brixton," as George Moore expresses it. England brings material prosperity when she sets her foot on a lesser nation, but it is generally accompanied by a waning of interest in the real things, which are the inward things—utilitarianism versus beauty, and a spiritual falling off, concealed by large religious machinery. Nowadays, when formerly the family would sing their own old songs, the vulgar strains of English music-hall ditties are heard, with a wretched accompaniment drummed out on a wretched instrument.

I have often wondered if the introduction of the cheap piano has anything to do with the decline of song as a means of expression amongst the people. Before the era of universal piano-playing, the people used to *think* music; and from thinking to expressing is but a step. They improvised little strains over their work, and by repetition and addition the little song grew unconsciously. Now, their ambition is to have a piano, and to have their children learn to play. "Learning music" to them means learning to play the piano, and so that unfortunate instrument has become to them, as to the vast majority, a substitute for music in the brain. I talk more of the townspeople in this regard, many of whom think it a mark of inferiority to confess acquaintance with their own songs, when they can have English music and a piano. Even the "educated" classes are lamentably ignorant of their own treasures of folk-music, forgetting that the true and vigorous in art can only evolve from a nation's own inheritance of poetry and song; everything else must be exotic and transient. William Butler Yeats in his *Celtic Twilight* speaks much of this: "Folk art is indeed," he says, "the oldest of the aristocracies of thought, and because it refuses what is passing and trivial, the merely clever and pretty, as certainly as the vulgar and insincere, and because it has gathered into itself the simplest and most unforgettable thoughts of the generations, it is the soil where all great art is rooted. Wherever it is spoken by the fireside, or sung by the roadside, or carved upon the lintel, appreciation of the arts that a single mind gives unity and design to spreads quickly when its hour is come."

Probably there is more latent music in the peasant people in the remote mountainous parts, and in the Western Isles, where pianos and harmoniums are little known, than anywhere else in the country. In these districts singing still constitutes part of the daily life of the people. They have songs for their different tasks: their sheiling song (*Oran Airidh*), dumping song in weaving (*Oran Luaidh*), crooning song (*Crònan*), boating song (*Iorram*). In the Isle of Iona, at evening milking-time can be heard the longing strains of *Colin's Cattle* (*Crodh Chaillean*) sung by some girlish voice; and fascinating is it in the long, sweet twilight, with the senses steeped in the most delicate, ethereal coloring, to listen to the quaint strains of a *Iorram* stealing across the calm waters of the Sound, as the boats come home. Neither England nor John Knox has been able to rob these people entirely of their beauty feeling, and so long as that is in their hearts, at any moment the needed touch can waken it into artistic expression. They love their mountains, their fields, their seas and lochs with a passionate love. The very first night of many I have spent in one of the Western Isles was one of those wonderful, dreamy, charmed evenings with a tender rosy light over everything. As I sat outside our cottage I noticed during the evening an old woman pass and repass, walking slowly with her knitting in her hand, but with eyes looking far away, out to sea and the distant hills. Once as she passed, she turned to me, and with a smile on her heavily wrinkled face, said, "God has made it so beautiful, I cannot go into my lonely room, and leave it all;" and then she stood beside me, quite silent, gazing with dreaming eyes across to the glowing rocks of Mull. The poor woman had had much trouble, as I afterwards learned, but the peace of that evening had passed into her. In this sense they are all poets by nature, sensitively alive to beauty, to whom inward life is more than material prosperity; therefore considered by many unprogressive and lazy. One old Gael, who used to sit on the rocks and have long "thinks" every day, said once to me, "The English say that we are lazy, but it will be because they do not understand us."

One reason for the Gaelic melodies being so little known outside of the Gaelic-speaking people is the difficulty of translating the verses into English without losing the peculiar flavor and the oneness with the music. Then the majority of the melodies have, until recently, been published only in little paper editions without accompaniment, or in large expensive ones. These little editions of the *Celtic Lyre*, edited by Mr. Henry Whyte ("Fionn") of Glasgow, and the *Songs of the Gael*, by Mr. Lachlan MacBean, in which the melodies are written as sung by the people, are in every cottage in the Highlands and Western Isles, and the long winter nights are spent in singing, seated round the glowing peat fires.

Many of the older songs were improvised by the bards to a harp accompaniment, and handed down by memory from generation to generation. The early kings had all their attendant harpers, as had also the Highland chiefs. One of the last, Murdoch MacDonald, died about 1736 in Quinish, Mull. A bard had not only to play and sing, but was expected to improvise on the exciting incidents of the time. This may explain, as has been suggested, the curious closes of many of the melodies, on different degrees of the scale, as between the verses a full close may have been avoided. This facility in verse-making is still a characteristic of the Scottish Gael. Every New Year's night, in certain parts, after the hour of midnight, the people visit one another, and standing on the threshold, recite original verses before entering.

Numbers of the more modern melodies owe their birth to the bagpipes, which superseded the harp within the last three hundred years. The piper to a chief was a highly important personage, who owned lands, and whose pipes were always carried for him by a servant. The Macrimmon family, who served the Macleods, were quite renowned. A school for pipers, founded by them, was for long in existence in the Isle of Skye, and contrary to the custom of most modern schools of music, "no pupil was admitted who had not an ear for music," fees being quite secondary in importance. It was one of the Macrimmon family who was daring enough to penetrate into a sea cave inhabited by the fairies. As he marched in, he played on his pipes, and his friends outside listened in awe as they heard the sounds becoming fainter and fainter, when suddenly his dog rushed out, panting with terror. His master never returned, though at times the sound of his pipes is heard.

Up to the middle of the nineteeth century, the pipers were the keepers of the old traditions, and every springtime and harvest they journeyed through the different districts, entertaining the people with their music and legends, in return for which they were generously welcomed and lodged. The shepherds also, in the solitudes of the mountains, had large stores in their memory of the warlike songs of their fathers. In those days, those who occupied themselves with music, even in the rudest and simplest way, never complained of bad memories! The songs and stories were in their hearts, that is all.

The reign of Queen Anne and those of the first two Georges were again prolific in Scottish song-making of the more modern types. Allan Ramsay, Lady Wardlaw, Lady Grizzel Baillie, Robert Crawford, and others lived in that time, and song, such as it was, was zealously cultivated by the aristocracy. It is told of Lady Murray, daughter of Lady Grizzel Baillie, that, in her evening assemblies in the Old Parliament Close, Edinburgh, she sang her native melodies, accompanying herself on the spinet, with such touching sweetness, that she rarely closed without a sympathetic sob from some of her hearers.

To the ancient Celt the study of music was a primary part of education. Bude tells us that at all the ancient entertainments the harp was passed round, and so great was the disgrace attached to any one who could not sing or play that the one who was conscious of inability generally disappeared before his turn came. At a funeral, a Coronach was indispensable; without it the soul would restlessly wander about the neighborhood of its earthly remains. Later, the bagpipes took the place of harps and voices at funerals, and now, with the decadence of Calvinism, these poetic customs are again being revived, although at present rather by exception than by rule.

In many of the mountainous parts the burying-places were islands out on the lochs, and one can well picture the scene as the boat containing the coffin glided over the quiet waters, while the mournful laments were echoed from the listening hills. Some years ago the funerals of Professor Blackie and Mrs. Mary MacKellar, a Gaelic poetess, were a revival of ancient customs in the city of Edinburgh; the coffins covered with tartan plaids, and strewn with heather, being carried shoulder-high by Highlanders through the streets, while the pipers marched in front, playing wild, weird laments. Two summers ago I witnessed a funeral in one of the Western Isles, where the coffin was carried by the mourners to a little boat, while all stood on the beach with uncovered heads, as it slowly sailed through the mist to one of the other islands. Everything was calm and beautiful, but I missed the final touch that would have been added by the wail of the pipes. For a chief they would have been played.

In Ireland, at the present day, more than in Scotland, they are seeking to revive the old legends, and preserve the ancient characteristics of the people. The Gaelic League, and the efforts of such men as Yeats, Douglas Hyde, A. E. (George Russell), and others, and such women as Lady Gregory, Lady Charlotte Guest, etc., are doing much to interest the Irish in their own history and traditions by the preservation in a literary form of the old legends and beliefs of the people. Scotland, also, has the exquisite writings of Fiona MacLeod, who has led us to far-off dreaming isles and rock-bound coasts, and allowed those who have the vision to see into the heart of the Gael, and to dream his dream. A sympathetic study of her works, and Mr. Alexander Carmichael's *Carmina Gadelica*, in which he has translated and preserved old runes, incantations, records of old customs, etc., will surely bring about a closer understanding of the Scottish Gael, his feelings and his aspirations.

And has not Edward MacDowell, in his later style, given unique and beautiful expression in music to the Celtic spirit? Celtic Scotland and Ireland may well claim him, although born in America, as the one who has most artistically expressed the old poetic atmosphere. In his *Celtic Sonata*, one feels wrapped in the elemental atmosphere of the old heroic times, with all the largeness, and pathos, and tragedy of ancient loves and wars. One feels something in his music that is born of the Celtic past; he has allowed his race to speak clearly through him. It seems a long way from

Scottish folk-song to Edward MacDowell's art music; but would it be fanciful to go a little further and say that I believe that no sensitive musical temperament, nourished from childhood on the old Gaelic songs, and musically developed on art lines later, could ever find the works of the most modern French composers incomprehensible or unsympathetic? The tonal characteristics of such music, the spirit of it, could not seem new and strange to such an one, but would appeal to him as something familiar, home-like, near.

I have dwelt more upon the Celtic music of Scotland because it is much less known than the Lowland, and I think has more musical significance and relation to art development. In a book arranged to give a general idea of Scottish folk-song, the best known Lowland airs had also to be included, but I hope that some, when searching for old favorites, will now and again meet with pleasant little surprises in these quaint old Gaelic songs, which surely they will come to love.

Very many widely different versions exist of all of the old Scottish melodies and verses, but I feel that the sources from which I have drawn present the best and most singable combinations. I should like to acknowledge the kindness of Mr. Alfred Moffat and his publishers, Messrs. Augener, who have permitted me to use many of his versions of the well-known airs and verses; also, the courtesy of Mr. Henry Whyte, of the *Celtic Lyre*, and Mr. Lachlan MacBean, of *Songs of the Gael*, who generously placed their Gaelic melodies and translations of verses at my disposal. My thanks are also due to Mr. Stronach, of the Advocates' Library, Edinburgh, for helping me to make acquaintance with many interesting old manuscripts and books bearing on the subject.

Boston, February, 1905.

Helen Hopekirk

GLOSSARY

a', all
aboot, about
ae, one
aft, aften, oft, often
Agam, mine
aik, oak
ain, own
amang, among
an', if
ance, once
ane, one
anither, another
aquent, acquainted
aught, anything
auld, old, *auld lang syne*, the good old times
awa', away
ay, constantly
aye, always
Bain, light-haired
bairn, bairnie, child
baith, both
banshee, a spirit that wails when a relative is about to die
bardies, poets
bark, boat
beld, bald
Ben, Mount
ben, mountain, hill; parlor; into the parlor
biggs, builds
bing'd, bowed
birken, birch
birkenshaw, birch wood
bit, bit of
blaeberries, bilberries
blawn, blown
bleer, dim
blenching, flinching
blink, glimpse
bluid, blood, *bluidy*, bloody
blythe, blithe
bobbit, curtsied
boding, foreboding
body, person, creature
'boon, above
bow'r, bower, arbor, private rooms
brae, hill, hillside
braid, broad
brak, broke
brake, fern
braw, fine, handsome, gaily dressed
brent, smooth
brows, slopes
burd, young lady
burnside, brookside
burstit, burst
but, in the outer room, *but and ben*, all around the house
bye, near
cam', came
canach, cotton grass (a sedge)
canna, cannot
cannie, fortunate, wise, pleasant
cannilie, prudently
canty, merry
carl, boor
cauld, cold
clamb, climbed
claymore, Highland sword
clead, dress
coo, cow
corrie, hollow in a hillside
cot, cottage
couldna, couldn't
couls, fellows (?)
crofts, small tenant farms
crouse, cheerful
crowd, put on extra sail
cuifs, dolts
daff, talk foolishly
daur, dare, *daurna*, dare not
dawt, caress
dee, die
deid, dead
de'il, deil, devil
dell, hollow, small valley
dhu, black-haired
dine, dinner
dinna, don't
dirk, dagger
dochter, daughter
donn, brown-haired
dool, woe, sorrow
doon, doun, down
dowie, sad
downa, cannot
drappin', dropping
dykeside, side of a fence
ebon, ebony
e'e, ee, eye
e'en, een, eyes
eerie, apprehensive
eile, another
ere, before
fa', fall, *fa's*, falls
fain, gladly, glad
fair, sweetheart

fairly, actually
falconet, small cannon
fareweel, farewell
fashious, bothersome
fauld, sheepfold
fause, false
fein, glad (?)
fetter, restraint
fere, comrade
ferlie, marvel
foot, step
forgat, forgot
fortochten, (a variant of, or error for, *forfochten,* "worn out"?)
frae, from
fu', full, very
Fye, fie (?)
gae, go
gaed, gave, went
ga'in, going
gane, gone
gang, go
gar, make
gat, got
gaucy, buxom
gaun, going
gear, wealth, goods
ghaist, ghost
gie, give, *gi'ed, gie'd,* gave, *gi'es,* give us
gin, 'gin, if
glen, valley
gloaming, twilight
gloom, become gloomy
Gorry, (?)
gowan, daisy
gowd, gold
greetin', weeping, crying
gude, good, *gude-willie,* good-will
gudeman, husband
gude's, good as
ha', hall
hadna, hadn't
hae, ha'e, have
hale, whole, entire
hame, home
haud, hold
heartsome, merry, cheerful
heathcocks, blackcocks
heeree, (an exclamation)
heugh, crag, steep bank
Hieland, highland
hilty-skilty, helter-skelter, capricious
hinny, honey
hó, (an exclamation)
hóro, (an exclamation)
Hóvan, (?)
howe, hollow
howkit, dug
i', in
ilka, every
I'se, I shall
ither, other
jinkin', frisking
jo, sweetheart
Kailyaird, kitchen garden
Kelpins, water sprites
ken, know
kilted, tucked up
kirk, church
knowes, knolls, small hills
kye, kine, cows
kythes, shows, appears
laigh, low
laird, landowner
lammie, little lamb
lane, lone, alone, *lanely,* lonely
lang, long
lauch, laugh
lave, (the) rest
law, low
lawfu', lawful
lays, songs
lea, pasture
leal, faithful, *land o' the leal,* heaven
leelang, livelong
licht, light, *licht's,* light as
lighted, alighted, dismounted
lightsome, graceful, merry
lilt, song
lo'e, love, *lo'ed,* loved
Loorgeen, stem, shaft (?; name of the boat?)
loot, let
lour, lower, darken, threaten
Mahoun, a name for the devil
mair, more
maist, most, almost
mak', make
'mang, among
mar tha mi, the way I am
marmalete, marmalade
maun, must
maut, malt
mavis, song thrush
meikle, much
mettled, spirited
Mhairi, Mary
mind, remember
Mess, Master
mi, I
minnie, mother
mirk, dark
mither, mother
mo, my
monie, mony, many
moorcock, red grouse

moss, bog
mou', mouth
muckle, great, big
muir, moor
muirhen, red grouse
muirlan', moor, moorland
mutch, cap
na, not, no
nae, no
naething, nothing
nane, none, no one
neen, maiden
ne'er, never
nicht, night
no', not
noo, now
och, Ochone, alas
o'ercome, refrain
òg, young
oor, our
owre, over, too
paidelt, paddled
palfrey, horse
pawky, saucy, lively
philabeg, kilt
pintstoup, pint flagon
plaidie, plaid (garment)
plenishing, furniture, stock
posie, nosegay
pow, head
pree'd, tasted
prick'd, goaded
pu', pull, pick, put
puir, poor
rade, rode
rarely, finely, copiously, with rare skill
reeks, smoke
richt, all right
rightfu', rightful
rill, brook
rin, run
routh, plenty
rova, (?)
rowan, rowanberry
row'd him, wrapped himself
Rùn, darling
sae, so
sair, sore, sorely, passionately
sall, shall
sang, song
sangster, songster
saut, salt
Scotia, Scotland
seamew, sea gull
shielins, cottages
sic, such
siller, silver
simmer, summer
sin', since
sma', small
snaw, snow
snawwreaths, snowdrifts
solan, solan goose
som, (?)
speer, spier, ask
stockdove, a wild pigeon
stown, stolen
straked, stroked
strathspey, a type of dance
'stu, you are
syne, then
tae, to
tak', take
tha, am (is, are)
thegither, together
thinkna ye, don't you think
thocht, thought
thorn, hawthorn
tine, lose
toun, town
trim, stabilize
trippit, tripped, stepped lightly
trode, trod
trow, think
twa, two
twin'd, robbed
wad, would
wadna, wouldn't
wae's, woe is
waefu', woeful
warldly, worldly
waught, draft (of ale)
waukin', waking
waur, worse
weal, happiness, well-being
weel, well
weir, war
wert, were
wha, wha', who
whar, where
wi', with
wile, estrange, beguile away
wilfu', willful
willie, will, *gude-willie,* good-will
winna, will not, won't
won, live, reside
wrack, wreck
wraith, ghost
wrang, wrong
yade, jade (broken-down horse)
yer, your
yestreen, last night
yett, gate
yowe, ewe

ADIEU, DUNDEE

Air from Skene MS (1630)
Accompaniment by HELEN HOPEKIRK

CHARLES NEAVES

tenderly
rit.
a tempo
In the light o' Ma - ry's e'e, Fair - est seem - ings
rit.
a tempo
maist be - guil - ing Love, a - dieu! a - dieu, Dun - dee.
f
f
p very quietly
Like yon wa - ter
f
sf
p
soft - ly glid - ing, When the winds are laid to sleep;

cresc.
Such _ my life, when I con - fid-ing Gave to her my
cresc.
heart _ to keep. Like _ yon wa - ter wild - ly rush - ing
f
f sf
sf
When _ the north-wind stirs _ the sea, Such _ the change my
p rit.
p rit.
heart now crush-ing, Love, a - dieu! a - dieu, _ Dun - dee.
f a tempo
rit.
f a tempo
rit.

AYE WAKIN', O!

First verse traditional
Second verse by ROBERT BURNS

Ancient Scottish Air
Accompaniment by HELEN HOPEKIRK

think on my bon - nie lad, An' bleer my een wi' greet - in',
wa - ter rins owre the heugh, And I long for my lov - er,
mf
p
Aye wak - in', O! Wak - in' aye an' eer - ie, Sleep I can - na get For
Aye wak - in', O! Wak - in' aye an' eer - ie, Sleep I can - na get For
f
think - in' on my dear - ie, Aye wak - in', O!
think - in' on my dear - ie, Aye wak - in', O!
p rit.
pp

A WEE BIRD CAM' TO OUR HA' DOOR
(WAE'S ME FOR PRINCE CHARLIE)

One of the versions of
Lady Cassilis Lilt (Skene MS)
Accompaniment by HELEN HOPEKIRK

WILLIAM GLEN (1789-1826)

cresc.
Char - lie!" Oh! when I heard the bon-nie, bon - nie bird, The
sor - row?" "Oh! no, no, no," the wee bird sang, "I've
dan - ger. Yes - treen I met him in a glen, My
cresc.
cresc.
tears cam' drap - pin' rare - ly, I took my bon - net
flown sin' morn - in' ear - ly, But sic a day o'
heart maist burst - it fair - ly, For sad - ly chang'd in -
cresc.
p espress.
rit.
off my head, For weel I lo'ed Prince Char - lie.
wind and rain, Oh! wae's me for Prince Char - lie.
deed was he, Oh! wae's me for Prince Char - lie.
p
rit.
a tempo

slightly quicker
f
4."Dark night came on, the tem - pest roar'd, Loud
5. But now the bird saw some red 'coats, An' he
f
o'er the hills and val - leys. An' where was't that your
shook his wings wi' an - ger, "Oh, this is no' a
Prince lay down, Wha's hame should been a pal - ace. He
land for me; I'll tar - ry here nae long - er!" He

row'd him_ in a High - land_ plaid, That cov - er'd him but
hov - er'd_ on the wing a - while, Ere he de-part - ed
pp rit.
spare - ly. An' slept be_ neath a bush_ o'_ broom, Oh!
fair - ly. But weel I mind the fare - weel_ strain, Was,
wae's me for_ Prince Char - lie!"
"Wae's me for_ Prince Char - lie!"
pp

AILIE BAIN O' THE GLEN
(EILIDH BHÀN)

From the Gaelic of
EVAN MAC COLL (The Lochfyne Bard)
Translated by Malcolm MacFarlane

Air from the "Celtic Lyre"
Accompaniment by HELEN HOPEKIRK

a tempo
CHORUS
Quick-ly come, my dear-ie.
I'd gang rhym-in' craz-y.
Ai-lie Bain o' the glen, Bon-nie las-sie, win-some las-sie;
a tempo
Ai-lie Bain o' the glen, Wha' could help but lo'e her?
SOLO
rit.
3. On the cauld nichts tho' my plaid-ie Shel-ter'd us but spare-ly,
4. What tho' mon-ied cuifs en-deav-or Wi' their gowd tae lure ye;
rit.

a tempo
Yet my part - in' frae be - side ye Seem'd tae come owre ear ly.
True tae me yer heart beats ev - er; Ne'er shall they se - cure ye!
a tempo
CHORUS
f
p
f
Al - lie Bain o' the glen, Bon-nie las-sie, win-some las - sie; Ai - lie Bain o' the glen,
f
p
f
Wha' could help but lo'e her?
f

BALOOLOO, MY LAMMIE

Air from "Grieg's Minstrelsy"
Accompaniment by HELEN HOPEKIRK

Lady CAROLINA NAIRNE (1766-1845)

ails my wee bairn-ie, what ails it this nicht? What
rock-in' fu' sweet-ly on mam-mie's warm knee, But
ails my wee bairn-ie, is bairn-ie no richt?
dad-die's a-rock-in' up-on the saut sea.
pp
pp
rit.
p
3. Now hush-a-ba,— lam-mie; Now hush-a, my dear; Now
4. Sing ba-loo, my lam-mie, Sing ba-loo, my dear; Sing
p a tempo

hush - a - ba, lam - mie, ain min-nie is here; The
ba - loo, my lam - mie, ain min-nie is here; My
wild wind is rav - in; and mam - mie's heart's sair; The
wee bairn - ie's doz - in', it's doz - in' now fine, And,
pp
rit.
wild wind is rav - in' And ye din - na care.
oh! may its wauk - in' be blyth - er than mine.
pp
rit.
a tempo
1.
last time
pp

BLYTHE, BLYTHE AND MERRY WAS SHE

Yar - row banks the bir - ken - shaw; But Phe - mie was a
smile was like a sim - mer morn; She trip - pit by the
o'er the Low - lands I hae been; But Phe - mie was the
bon - nier lass, Than braes o' Yar - row ev - er saw.
banks o' Earn, As licht's a bird up - on a thorn.
blyth - est lass, That ev - er trod the dew - y green.
CHORUS
f
Blythe, blythe and mer - ry was she, Blythe was she but and ben,
Blythe by the banks o' Earn, And blythe in Glen - tur - rit glen.
Repeat from 𝄋

BY THE STREAM SO PURE AND CLEAR
(SONG OF THE ISLE OF SAINT KILDA)

From "Johnson's Museum"
Accompaniment by HELEN HOPEKIRK

f a tempo
where shall I — the youth dis - cov - er?
f a tempo
mf
Keeps he in your breez - y shade, Ye rocks and moss and i - vy wav - ing,
mf
On some bank where wild waves lav - ing Mur - mur through the twist - ed wil - low?
p
p
pp tenderly
rit.
On that bank, oh, were I laid, How soft should be — my lov - er's — pil - low!
pp
rit.

BY YON BONNIE BANKS

*) Traditional Scottish Ballad

Old Melody: source unknown
Accompaniment by HELEN HOPEKIRK

*) Lady John Scott has stated that she and Sir John picked up both words and air from a poor little boy, who was singing in the streets of Edinburgh.

a tempo
Lo - mond! O, ye'll tak' the high road, An' I'll tak' the low road, An'
f a tempo
marcato
I'll be in Scot - land a - fore ye; But me an' my true love will
p
rit.
nev-er meet a-gain On the bon-nie, bon-nie banks o' Loch Lo-mond! 'Twas
Expressively
mp
there that we part-ed in yon shad-y glen, On the steep, steep side o' Ben Lo - mond, Where
cresc.
fz

dim.
f
in pur-ple hue the Hie-land hills we view, And the moon looks out frae the gloam - in'. O,
dim.
f
Ped.
a tempo
marcato
p
ye'll tak' the high road, an' I'll tak' the low road, an I'll be in Scot-land a - fore ye: But
a tempo
rit.
me an' my true love will nev-er meet a-gain On the bon-nie, bon-nie banks o Loch Lo-mond!
rit.
a tempo
The wild bird-ies sing and the wild flowers spring, And in sun-shine the wa-ters are
p

p
rit.
dim.
sleep-ing; But the brok-en heart it kens nae sec-ond spring, Tho' the
p
rit.
waefu' may cease frae their greet-in' O, ye'll tak' the high road, an'
dim.
a tempo
cresc.
p
I'll tak' the low road, An' I'll be in Scot-land a-fore ye; But
rit.
me an' my true love will nev-er meet a-gain, On the bon-nie, bon-nie banks o' Loch Lo-mond!
p
rit.

CAM' YE BY ATHOLL

Lang hast thou loved and trust - ed us fair - ly! Char - lie, Char - lie,
wha wad - na fol - low thee, King o' the High - land hearts, bon - nie Prince Char - lie.
f
3. I'll to Loch-iel and Ap - pin and kneel to them Down by Lord Mur - ray, and
4. Down through the Low - lands, down wi' the Whig - a - more, Loy - al true High - land - ers,

Roy of Kil - dar - lie; Brave Mac - in - tosh he shall fly to the field with them,
down wi' them rare - ly. Ron - ald and Don - ald, drive on, wi' the broad clay - more,
rit.
These are the lads I can trust wi' my Char - lie.
O - ver the reeks o' the foes o' Prince Char - lie.
f a tempo
Fol - low thee, fol - low thee,
sf a tempo
sf
wha wad - na fol - low thee? Lang hast thou loved and trust - ed us fair - ly! Char - lie, Char - lie,
wha wad - na fol - low thee, King o' the High - land hearts, bon - nie Prince Char - lie.

COME, ALL YE JOLLY SHEPHERDS
(WHEN THE KYE COME HAME)

p
kye come hame, when the kye come hame, 'Tween the gloam - in' and the mirk, when the
a tempo f
sf
p
rit.
mf
kye come hame.
3. See — yon-der pawk-y shepherd that
4. Then — since all na-ture joins in this
rit.
a tempo
sf
mf
rit.
a tempo
rit.
lin-gers on the hill, His — ewes are in the fauld and his lambs are ly - in' still; Yet he
love with - out al - loy, Oh, — wha would prove a trai - tor to na-ture's dear-est joy! Or —
rit.
a tempo
rit.

a tempo
rit.
p a tempo
dow - na gang to rest, for his heart is in a flame to meet his bon-nie las-sie, when the
wha would choose a crown, Wi' its per - ils and its fame, And miss his bon-nie las-sie, when the
a tempo
p
kye come hame! When the kye come hame, when the kye come hame, 'Tween the
kye come hame!
rit. a tempo f
mf
gloam-in'and the mirk, when the kye come hame.
sf

COPE SENT A LETTER FRAE DUNBAR
(JOHNNIE COPE)

Old Scottish Air
Accompaniment by HELEN HOPEKIRK

John-nie Cope, are ye wauk-in' yet? Or are your drums a - beat - in' yet? If
ye were wauk - in', I wad wait, To go to the couls i' the
morn - ing.
rit.
a tempo
4. When John - nie Cope he heard of this, He
5. Fye, John - nie, now get up and rin, The
6. When John - nie Cope to Ber - wick cam', They
sf
Ped.

thocht it wad - na be a - miss To have a horse in
High - land bag - pipes mak' a din; It's best to sleep in a
speer'd at him, Where's a' your men?" The de'il con-found me,
Mockingly
read-i-ness To flee a - wa' i' the morn - ing.
hale skin, For'twill be a bluid-y morn - ing.
'gin I ken, For I left them a' i' the morn - ing.
Hey, John-nie Cope, are ye
sf
wauk - in' yet Or are your drums a - beat - in' yet: If
rit.
a tempo
ye were wauk - in' I wad wait To go to the couls i' the morn - ing.
rit.
a tempo
sf

CRO-CHALLAIN WOULD GIE ME
(COLIN'S CATTLE)

From the Old Gaelic
Translated by C. M. P.

Old Highland Melody
From the "Celtic Lyre"
Accompaniment by HELEN HOPEKIRK

cresc.
Chal - lain are bon - nie, Cro - Chal - lain are braw, Like the wing o' the muir - hen Brown - spot - ted an' a'.
Chal - lain sae can - nie, In the heat o' the day, They lie 'mang the heath - er, While their calves 'round them play.
cresc.
Ped.
p
3 There's a load on my bos - om; There's a tear in my
4 Nae sleep - in', nae sleep - in', Nae sleep - in' for
p

ee; I am wae and for - toch - ten; There's nae
me Till they come that I'm seek - in, I maun
sleep - in' for me. Cro - Chal - lain are bon - nie, Cro -
ne'er close an ee. Cro - Chal - lain sae bon - nie, Cro -
cresc.
cresc.
Chal - lain are braw; Like the wing o' the muir - hen Brown -
Chal - lain sae dear; They aye fill the milk - pail, What
spot - ted an' a'.
braw calves they rear.

FAREWELL TO LOCHABER

(LOCHABER NO MORE)

a tempo
been; For Loch - a - ber no more, Loch - a - ber no
mind; Tho' loud - est of thun - ders on loud - er waves
fuse? With - out it, I ne'er can have mer - it for
p
a tempo
Ped.
more, We'll may - be re - turn to Loch - a - ber no
roar, That's nae - thing like leav - ing my love on the
thee, And los - ing thy fav - our I'd bet - ter not
rit.
rit.
a tempo
more. These tears that I shed they are a' for my dear, And
shore. To leave thee be - hind me my heart is sore pain'd, But by
be. I gae then, my lass, to win hon - our and fame, And
a tempo

cresc.
no— for the dan-gers at-tend-ing on— weir; Tho' bore on rough
ease that's in-glor-ious no— fame can be— gain'd; And beau-ty and
if— I should chance to come glo-rious-ly— hame, I'll bring— a—
f
cresc.
Ped.
seas— to a— far— blood-y— shore, May-be to— re-turn to Loch-
love's— the re— ward of the— brave, And I maun de-serve it be-
heart to thee with love— run-ning o'er,— And then I'll— leave thee and Loch-
p
rit.
a-ber no— more.
fore I can— crave.
a-ber no— more.
pp
rit.
Ped.

FAR OVER YON HILLS
(FLORA MACDONALD'S LAMENT)

JAMES HOGG (1770-1835)
(The Ettrick Shepherd)

Air by NIEL GOW
Accompaniment by HELEN HOPEKIRK

rit.
a tempo cresc.
dew on her plaid, an' the tear_ in her e'e. She look'd_ at a boat wi' the
aw'd and un-hunt-ed his ey-rie can claim. The so-lan can sleep on the
red is the sword of the stran-ger and slave. The hoof_ of the horse and the
rit.
a tempo cresc.
breez-es that swung,_ A-way on the waves like a
shelf of the shores;_ The cor-mo-rant roost on his
foot of the proud,_ Have trode o'er the plumes on the
rit. p
bird on the main;_ An' ay as it les-sen'd she sigh'd as she sung, "Fare-
rock of the sea;_ But ah! there is one whose hard fate I de-plore, Nor
bon-net of blue;_ Why slept the red bolt in the breast of the cloud When
rit. p

a tempo
f marcato
weel to the lad I shall ne'er see a - gain! Fare - weel to my he - ro, the
house, ha', nor hame in his coun-try has he, The con - flict is past and our
ty - ran-ny rev - ell'd in blood of the true? Fare - weel my young he - ro, the
a tempo
f
gal - lant and young, Fare - weel to the lad I shall
name is no more, There's nought left but sor - row for
gal - lant and good! The crown of thy fa - thers is
p
sf
p
rit.
1. & 2.
last time
ne'er see a-gain!"
Scot-land and me!
torn from thy brow!
a tempo
rit.
p

FLOW GENTLY, SWEET AFTON

(AFTON WATER)

ROBERT BURNS (1759-1796)

Composer of air unknown
Accompaniment by HELEN HOPEKIRK

Burns sent the air with his poem to Johnson for the "Scot's Museum."

mur - mur - ing stream, Flow gen - tly, sweet Af - ton, dis -
scream - ing for - bear, I charge you, dis - turb not my
turb not her dream.
slum - ber - ing fair.
mp
3. How
p
Ped. * Ped. * Ped. *
loft - y, sweet Af - ton, thy neigh - bour - ing hills Far
mark'd with the cours - es of sweet wind - ing rills! There

cresc.
rit.
daily I wander as morn rises high, My
cresc.
rit.
a tempo
flocks and my Mary's sweet cot in my eye.
a tempo
p
4. Flow gently, sweet Afton, a-
p
p
mong thy green braes, Flow gently, sweet

p
riv - er, the theme of my lays; My
Ma - ry's a - sleep by thy mur - mur - ing
rit.
stream, Flow gen - tly sweet Af - ton, dis -
turb not her dream.
pp
Ped.

GIN A BODY MEET A BODY
(COMIN' THRO' THE RYE)

ROBERT BURNS (1759-1796)

Old Scottish Air
Accompaniment by HELEN HOPEKIRK

f a tempo
rit. dim.
a tempo
Il - ka las-sie has her lad-die, Nane they say — ha'e I; Yet
Il - ka las-sie has her lad-die, Ne'er a ane — ha'e I; But
Il - ka las-sie has her lad-die, Nane they say — ha'e I; But
f
rit.
cresc.
p
a' the lads they smile to me, When com-in' thro' the rye.
a' the lads they smile on me, When com-in' thro' the rye.
a' the lads they lo'e me weel, And what the waur am I?
a tempo
p
rit.
pp
mf a tempo
p a tempo

HAME, HAME, HAME!

Original Version
by ALLAN CUNNINGHAM (1784-1842)

Old Air
Accompaniment by HELEN HOPEKIRK

flow'r is in the bud, and the leaf up-on the tree, The lark shall sing me hame to my
ain coun-trie.
L.H.
p
mp
Hame, hame, hame, O —
hame fain — wad I be —
cresc.
Hame, hame, hame to my ain coun - trie! The green
L.H.
p
cresc.

cresc.
leaf o' loy-al-tie is be-gin-ning for to fa', And the bon-nie white rose it is
cresc.
f enthusiastically
with-er-ing and a! But I'll wa-ter't wi' the bluid o' u-surp-ing tyr-an-nie, And
f
green it will grow in my ain coun-trie.
L.H.
f
pp
Hame, hame, hame, O hame fain wad I be,
3
pp

p sadly
Hame, hame, hame to my ain coun - trie! The great now are gane, a' who
ven-tur'd for to save, And the new grass is grow-ing a - bove their bluid-y grave, But the
rit.
cresc.
sun in the mirk blinks blythe in my e'ee, I'll
shine on ye yet in yer ain coun - trie.
p
mf
L.H.
pp

HEAVY THE BEAT OF THE WEARY WAVES

(OLD DIRGE FROM THE ISLE OF MULL)

p
one. Tears of de - spair from the
p
weep - ing sky, Fall - ing to the earth be-neath, And o'er the gloom-y
pp
heath Hangs a mist - y pall of death, of death! Och-one! Ev -
pp
rit.
- - er more, Och - one!
rit.
p a tempo

HUSH-A-BY, DARLING

The verses by Lachlan MacBean
are relics of an old Lochaber Lullaby

Ancient Lochaber Lullaby
from "Songs of the Gael"
Accompaniment by HELEN HOPEKIRK

Tenderly

p a tempo
3. Soft - ly and si - lent - ly eye - lids are clos - ing, Dear - est wee
4. Plac - id - ly, peace - ful - ly, slum - ber has bound him, An - gels are
a tempo
jew - el, so gen - tly he's doz - ing; Soft - ly he's rest - ing, by
lov - ing - ly watch - ing a - round him; Beau - ti - ful spir - its, his
p
slum - ber o'er - tak - en, Sound - ly he's sleep - ing, and sweet - ly he'll
sor - row be - guil - ing, Sweet - ly they whis - per, and ba - by is
dim.
rit.
pp
wak - en.
smil - ing.
1.
2.
a tempo
pp rit.
pp

HUSH YE, MY BAIRNIE
(CAGARAN GAOLACH)

Old Gaelic (Lochaber) Lullaby
Translated by Malcolm MacFarlane

From the "Celtic Lyre"
Accompaniment by HELEN HOPEKIRK

p
Hush ye, my bairn - ie my
p a tempo
p
bon - nie wee lam - mie; Routh o' guid things ye shall
rit.
bring tae yer mam - mie; Hare frae the mea - dow, and
p a tempo
rit.
p a tempo
deer frae the moun - tain, Grouse frae the muir - lan', and

trout frae the foun - tain.
p
Hush ye, my bairn - ie, my bon - nie wee dear - ie, Sleep! come and close the een
pp
Ped.
rit.
heav - y and wear - ie; Closed are the wear - ie een, rest ye are tak - in',
pp
ppp
Sound be yer sleep - in', and bright be yer wak - in'.

I CLIMB THE MOUNTAINS
(FHIR A BHÀTA)

Translated from the Gaelic
by Lachlan MacBean

Old Gaelic Air
From the "Celtic Lyre"
Accompaniment by HELEN HOPEKIRK

boat - man, na hó - ro ei - le, O my boat - man, na hó - ro ei - le, O my
f
boat - man, na hó - ro ei - le,_ Joy a - wait thee when-e'er thou sail-est!
cresc. sf
Ped.
mf
3. My lov - er pro - mis'd to bring his la - dy A silk - en
4. I may not hide it_ my heart's de - vo - tion Is not a
5. My heart is wear - y with cease - less wail - ing Like wound - ed
mf
gown and a tar - tan plaid - ie A ring of gold which would show his
sea - son's_ brief e - mo - tion; Thy love in child - hood be - gan to
swan when her strength is fail - ing Her notes of an - guish the lake a -
sf

sem - blance; But oh! I fear me for his re - mem - brance,
seize me, And ne'er shall fade un - til death re - lease me.
wak - en, By all her com - rades at last for - sak - en.
O, my
boat - man, na hó - ro ei - le, O my boat - man, na hó - ro
ei - le, O my boat - man, na hó - ro ei - le, Joy a -
wait thee when - e'er thou sail - est!
mf
f
cresc.
f
f
f

I LEFT MY DARLING LYING HERE

*)(A FAIRY LULLABY)

(AN COINEACHAN)

Old Gaelic Verses
Translated by Lachlan MacBean

From the "Celtic Lyre"
Accompaniment by HELEN HOPEKIRK

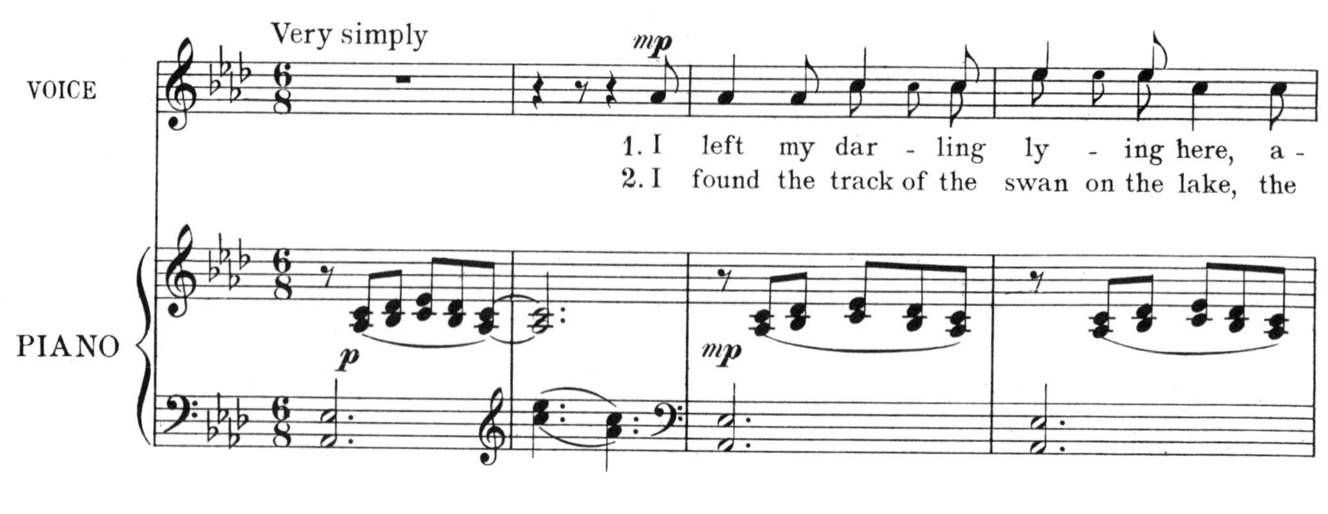

*) Sung by a mother whose child was stolen by the fairies.

mf
found the wee brown ot-ter's track, the ot-ter's track, the ot-ter's track, I've
found the track of the yel-low fawn, the yel-low fawn, the yel-low fawn, I
mf
p rit.
found the wee brown ot-ter's track But ne'er a trace o' ba-by, O!
found the track of the yel-low fawn But could not trace my ba-by, O!
p rit.
mp
3. I
a tempo
rit.
found the trail of the moun-tain mist, the moun-tain mist, the moun-tain mist; I
a tempo

p
rit.
found the trail of the moun - tain mist, But ne'er a trace of
p
rit.
a tempo
ba - by, O! Hó - van, Hó - van Gor - ry òg O,
a tempo
Gor - ry òg O, Gor - ry òg O, Hó - van, Hó - van,
rit.
Gor - ry òg O, I've lost my dar - ling ba - by, O.
rit.

I'M WEARIN' AWA', JEAN

(THE LAND O' THE LEAL)

The original poem by
Lady Carolina Nairne (1766-1845)
(Robert Burns' version)

A version of an old air
"Hey, tuttie, tattie"
Accompaniment by HELEN HOPEKIRK

cresc.
nae sor - row there, Jean, There's nei - ther cauld nor care, Jean, The
bon- nie bairn's there, Jean, She was baith gude and fair, Jean, And,
p
rit.
day's aye fair I' the land o' the leal.
oh! we grudg'd her sair To the land o' the leal.
pp
rit.
a tempo
With animation
mf
3. But dry that tear-fu' ee Jean, Grieve
mf

cresc.
na for her and me, Jean, Frae sin and sor - row free I' the
cresc.
p
poco
land o' the leal. Now fare ye weel, my ain Jean! This warld's cares are
p
poco
dim.
rit.
pp
vain, Jean, We'll meet and aye be fein I' the land o' the leal.
dim.
rit.

I WISH I WERE WHERE HELEN LIES

(FAIR HELEN OF KIRKCONNEL)

Old Ballad

Ancient Air
Accompaniment by HELEN HOPEKIRK

f
accel.
Cursed be the heart that thought the thought And
mf
cursed the hand that fired the shot When in my arms burd Hel-en dropt, And
rit.
rit.
dim.
died to suc-cor me.
a tempo
p
But
dim.
pp
think-na ye my heart was sair When my love dropt down_ and spake nae mair There
p a tempo

did she swoon wi' mei-kle care On fair Kirk-con-nel
Lea.
p
I
p
longingly
wish I were where Hel-en lies, For night and day on me she cries, And
pp
I am wear - y of the skies For her sake that died for me.
rit.
rit.
pp

JOHN ANDERSON, MY JO, JOHN

*) Formerly used as a Roman Catholic Church Melody in Scotland before the Reformation.

mp
John An-der-son, my jo, John, We clamb the hill the-
a tempo
mf
Ped.
gith-er And mo-ny a can-ty day, John, We've had wi' ane an-
cresc.
cresc.
dolce
ith-er Now we maun tot-ter down, John, But hand in hand we'll
p
sempre dim. e rit.
go; And sleep the-gith-er at the foot, John An-der-son, my jo.
sempre dim. e rit.

MAXWELLTON BRAES ARE BONNIE

(ANNIE LAURIE)

Verses and Melody
by Lady JOHN SCOTT
Accompaniment by HELEN HOPEKIRK

me her prom - ise true, Which ne'er for - got will be, And for
e'er the sun shone on, And dark blue is her e'e, And for
f
bon - nie An - nie Lau - rie, I'd lay me doon an'
bon - nie An - nie Lau - rie, I'd lay me doon an'
rit.
dim.
rit.
dee.
dee.
a tempo
p
3. Like dew on the gow - an ly - ing Is the fa' o' her fair - y
p
pp

feet; And like winds in sum - mer sigh - ing Her
voice is low and sweet; Her voice is low and sweet, She's
a' the world to me, And for bon - nie An - nie Lau - rie, I'd
lay me doun an' dee.
p
rit.
rit.
pp

MY BROWN-HAIRED MAIDEN
(MO NIGHEAN DONN, BHÒIDHEACH)

Verses from the Gaelic
Translated by Lachlan MacBean

Old Gaelic Melody
From "Songs of the Gael"
Accompaniment by HELEN HOPEKIRK

.fair - - est, The beau - ty that thou bear - est, Thy
near thee, To see thee and to hear thee, These
swell - - ing, My dar - ling has her dwell - ing, A
witch - ing smile, the rar - est, Are ev - - er with me.
mem'-ries still en - dear thee For - ev - - er to me.
fair wild rose ex - cel - ling In sweet - ness is she.
After 3d verse
Ho - ro, my brown-haired maid - en, Hee - ree, my bon - nie maid - en, My
sweet - est, neat - est maid - en, I'll wed none but thee.

MY LOVE, SHE'S BUT A LASSIE YET

JAMES HOGG (1770-1835)
(The Ettrick Shepherd)

Old Scottish Air
Accompaniment by HELEN HOPEKIRK

f
there's a braw time com-in' yet, When we may gang a-roam-in' yet, An'
hint wi' glee O' joys to be, When fa's the mod-est gloam-in' yet.
rit.
p a tempo
She's
nei-ther proud nor sau-cy yet, She's nei-ther plump nor gau-cy yet; But
mp

just a jink-in', Bon-nie blink-in', Hil - ty - skil-ty las-sie yet. But
O! her art-less smile's mair sweet, Than hin-ny or than mar-ma - lete, An'
right or wrang E'er it be lang, I'll bring her to a par-ley yet.
p
p
I'm

expressively
rit.
a tempo
jeal-ous o' what bless - es her, The ver-y breeze that kiss-es her: The
p
rit.
a tempo
rit.
a tempo
flow-'ry beds on which she treads, Tho' wae— for— ane that miss - es her. Then
rit.
a tempo
O! to meet my las - sie yet, Up— in that glen so grass-y yet, For—
rit.
a tempo
all I see are nought to me Save her— that's but a las - sie yet.
rit.
a tempo

MY LOVE TO MY BRIDE

(FAIR YOUNG MARY)

(MÀIRI BHÀN ÒG)

From the Gaelic of D (Bàn) Mc Intyre*
Translated by Lachlan MacBean

Melody from "Songs of the Gael"
Accompaniment by HELEN HOPEKIRK

*) To his newly wedded wife.

a tempo
grown. My thoughts used to rove in boy - ish fol - ly Ere
hue: That bough from a - bove, de - sir - ing great-ly, With
a tempo
ev - er her love I had known, But now I'm her own, my
love un - to me I drew; None else could have mov'd that
heart is whol - ly My dar - ling's a - lone, a - lone.
tree so state - ly 'Twas on - ly for me that it grew.
rit.
pp
R.H.
L.H.

MY OWN DEAR ONE'S GONE

(DH' FHALBH MO LEANNAN FHÉIN)

From the Gaelic of "Fionn" (Henry Whyte)
Translated by A. M. Rose

Old Gaelic Air
From the "Celtic Lyre"
Accompaniment by HELEN HOPEKIRK

Naught re-main'd but sad-ness; Till thou come a-gain I can ne'er know glad-ness.
Pierc-ing like an ar-row, That be-neath the wave Sleeps "my win-some mar-row."
rit.
My own dear one's gone.
My own dear one's gone.
rit.
p
Ped.
Ped.
after 2nd verse
Sad the tale to me; Need I long-er tar-ry? Death, to rest, and thee,
p
rit.
rit.
Soon my soul will car-ry. My own dear one's gone!
rit.
rit.

MY BROWN MAID

(MO NIGHEAN DONN)

From the Gaelic
Translated by C.M.P.

Air from the "Celtic Lyre"
Accompaniment by HELEN HOPEKIRK

SOLO
Roll the crest-ed waves hoar-y to the shore with weird moan - ing Mo
neen donn.
CHORUS
f a tempo
Sing-ing hó, ro-va hó, Let's be go-ing Mo neen donn.
L.H.
SOLO
p
In the woods the sweet sing-ers un-der wing their heads stow them Mo
rit.
neen donn.
CHORUS
a tempo
Sing-ing hó, ro-va hó, Let's be go-ing Mo neen donn.
rit.
a tempo
p

SOLO
mp
rit.
In the land of old Os-sian, my sad loss I'm de - plor - ing Mo
mp
CHORUS
a tempo
neen donn. Sing-ing hó, ro-va hó Let's be go - ing Mo neen donn.
L.H.
a tempo
SOLO
very slowly
p
Where I left — her, my dear one, my own peer-less a - dor'd one Mo
p
L.H.
R.H.
R.H.
CHORUS
f a tempo
neen donn. Sing-ing hó, ro-va hó Let's be go - ing Mo neen donn.
a tempo
f

MY PRETTY MARY

(MÀIRI BHÒIDHEACH)

From Sinclair's "Oranaiche"
Translated by C. M. P.

Old Melody of the Hebrides
From the "Celtic Lyre"
Accompaniment by HELEN HOPEKIRK

sun - shine, wher - e'er I wan - der, My wont is on thy charms to
has of joy be - reft me, And nought but sor - row now is
pon - der; Thy im - age ris - es up be - fore me, And throws love's
left me; From day to day 'tis sigh - ing, pin - ing, For thy sweet
witch - ing gla - mour o'er me.
face like a sun - beam shin - ing.
D.S.
L.H.
3. Who ev - er saw thee but felt thy pow - er? Of Beau - ty's

handmaids thou art the flow-er; And sense and worth, all else ex-cel - ling, With-in thy
rall.
a tempo
vir - tu-ous mind are dwell-ing. O ne'er may e - vil chance come
rall.
a tempo
near thee, With grief or gloom - y doubts to fear thee, But pleas-ant hopes and mus-ings
thine be, To cheer the days_ un-til thou mine be.
L.H.

NAE MAIR WE'LL MEET AGAIN

Highland Melody: "Robi donna Gorach"
Accompaniment by HELEN HOPEKIRK

O'ER COOLIN'S FACE THE NIGHT IS CREEPING

(MacCRIMMON'S LAMENT)

Translated from the Gaelic
by Lachlan MacBean

From "Songs of the Gael"
Accompaniment by HELEN HOPEKIRK

*) The verses were written on the departure of Donald MacCrimmon, piper to the MacLeods, in the year 1745 by his sister; the melody was composed for the same occasion.

CHORUS
with emphasis
mf
No more, no more, no more re - turn-ing, In peace nor in war is
he re - turn-ing; Till dawns the great day of doom and burn-ing, Mac -
Crim - mon is home no more re - turn-ing.
rit.
a tempo

p
4. We'll see no more Mac - Crim-mon's re-turn - ing In peace nor in war is
p
cresc.
he re-turn - ing Till dawns the great day of woe and burn - ing, For
cresc.
dim. rit.
him, for him there's no re - turn - ing.
rit.

OH, CHARLIE IS MY DARLING

Lady CAROLINA NAIRNE (1766-1845)

Old Melody
Accompaniment by HELEN HOPEKIRK

Char - lie came to our town, The young Che - va - lier.
a' the folks cam' rin - nin out, To meet the Che - va - lier.
cam' to fight for Scot-land's right, And the young Che - va - lier.
Oh,
Char-lie is my dar - ling, my dar - ling, my dar - ling! Char-lie is my dar - ling, the
young Che - va - lier.

4. They've left their bon-nie Hie-land hills, Their wives and bairn-ies dear, To draw the sword for Scot-land's lord, The gay Che-va-lier.
5. Oh, there were mon-y beat-ing hearts, And mon-y hope and fear, And mon-y were the pray'rs put up For the young Che-va-lier.
Oh, Char-lie is my dar-ling, my dar-ling, my dar-ling, my dar-ling! Char-lie is my dar-ling, the young Che-va-lier.
f
sf

O HEARKEN, AND I WILL TELL YOU HOW
(SCOTTISH WEDDING)

West of Scotland Melody
Accompaniment by HELEN HOPEKIRK

ROBERT BURNS (1759-1796)

truth I tell to you. But aye he cries "What-
meik-le mirth and glee. Out owre yon moss, out
sic a lad as ye." The woo-er he stepp'd
a tempo
sf
rit.
a tempo
e'er be-tide Mag-gie I'se hae to be my bride,"
owre yon muir, Till he cam to her dad-die's door,
up the house, And wow but he was won-drous crouse,
With a
rit.
fal-da-ra, fal-lal-da-ra, la-fal-lal-da-ra, lal-da-ra-la!
sf a tempo
sf
mp
4. The maid-en blush'd, and bing'd fu' law She had na will to say him na, But
5. The brid-al day it cam' to pass, Wi' mon-y a blythesome lad and lass; But
mp

to her dad-die she left it a' As they twa could a - gree. The
sic a day there nev-er was, Sic mirth was nev-er seen. This
sf
lov-er gie'd her then a kiss, Syne ran to her dad-die and tell'd him this,
win-some cou-ple strak-ed hands, Mess John tied up the mar-riage bands,
With a
rit.
a tempo
rit.
fal-da-ra, fal-lal-da-ra, la-fal-lal-da-ra, lal-da-ra-la!
sf a tempo
a tempo sf
1.
2.

OCH, OCH, MAR THA MI!

(THE ISLAY MAIDEN)

Translated from the Gaelic by Thomas Pattison (1828-1865)

Ancient Melody of Islay
From the "Celtic Lyre"
Accompaniment by HELEN HOPEKIRK

3. A - las, thy
4. Since thou hast
rit.
a tempo
kind eye, so bright - ly shin - ing; Thy neck so come - ly like ca-nach
left me, and with - out warn - ing, A - las, and tak - en a man for
blow - ing; Those eb - on eye - brows thy fore-head lin - ing; Thy cheeks like
gold! Had I been by thee, false wis - dom scorn - ing, Thy - self, my
rit.
ber - ries or row - ans blow - ing.
dear one, thou had'st not sold.
rit.
dim.

OH, LOVE WILL VENTURE IN

ROBERT BURNS (1759 - 1796)

West of Scotland Melody
Accompaniment by HELEN HOPEKIRK

rit.
mp
a tempo
ain dear May. I'll pu' the bud-ding rose-bush, when Phoe-bus peeps in view, For it's
ain dear May. I'll tie the po-sie round wi' the silk-en cord o' love, An' I'll
rit.
mp a tempo
Ped.
like a balm-y kiss o' her sweet bon-ny mou'; The hy-a-cinth's for con-stan-cy, wi'
place it in her breast, An' I'll swear by all a-bove, That to my lat-est breath o' life the
p
p
rit.
its un-chang-ing blue, An'___ a' to be a po-sie for my ain dear May.
band shall ne'er re-move; An'___ a' to be a po-sie for my ain dear May.
rit.

OH, MIRK, MIRK IS THE MIDNIGHT HOUR
(LORD GREGORY)

ope thy door! An ex - - ile
gi'e me rest? Ye mut - - t'ring
p
a tempo
rit.
p
frae her fa - - ther's ha', An' a' for
thun - ders from a - bove, Your will - - ing
lov - - ing thee; At least some pit - y
vic - - tim see! But spare and par - don
on me shaw If love it may na be!
my fause love His wrangs to heav'n and me!
rit.
dim.
rit. dim.
pp

OH, WHERE, TELL ME WHERE
(THE BLUE BELLS OF SCOTLAND)

Verses from
"Johnson's Museum"

Popular Scottish Air
Accompaniment by HELEN HOPEKIRK

ban - ners, where no - ble deeds are done; And it's
bon - net wi' bon - nie yel - low hair, And there's
wed us, And a clerk to say 'A - men!' And I'll
rit.
dim.
oh! in my heart I wish him safe at
nane in the world can wi' my love com -
ne'er part a - gain From my bon - nie High - land -
rit.
home."
pare."
man."
p a tempo

OH, MY LOVE IS LIKE A RED, RED ROSE

ROBERT BURNS (1759-1796)

Old Scottish Song
Accompaniment by HELEN HOPEKIRK

cresc.
fair art thou, my bon-nie lass, So deep in love am I; And
rit.
a tempo
I will love thee still, my dear, Till a' the seas gang dry.
dim.
mf
Till a' the seas gang dry, my dear, And the rocks melt wi' the sun: Oh, I will love thee still, my dear, While the

rit.
sands o' life shall run. And fare thee weel, my on-ly love! And
rit.
rit.
fare thee weel a-while! And I will come a-gain, my love, Tho'
rit.
a tempo
a tempo
't were ten thou-sand miles! Oh, my love is like a red, red rose, that's
p
p
new-ly sprung in June; Oh, my love's like the mel-o-die that's sweet-ly play'd in tune.
p
sf

OH, WHY LEFT I MY HAME?

R. GILFILLAN

Air adapted by PETER MACLEOD (1797-1859)
Accompaniment by HELEN HOPEKIRK

cresc.
sigh for Sco - tia's shore, And I gaze a - cross the
ty - rant's voice is here, And the wail of sla - ver -
cresc.
p rit.
sea, But I can - na get a blink O' my ain coun - trie!
ie; But the sun of Free - dom shines, In my ain coun - trie!
rit.
p
mf
3. There's a hope for ev - 'ry

woe, And a balm for ev - 'ry pain, But the first joys of our
heart Come never back a - gain. There's a track up-on the
deep, And a path a - cross the sea, But the
pp
pp
wear - ie ne'er re - turn To their ain coun - trie.
rit.
rit.

PUT OFF, AND ROW WI' SPEED

ROBERT ALLAN (1774-1841)

Highland Boat Song
Accompaniment by HELEN HOPEKIRK

Scot - land's Queen be a war - der's mark! Yon light that plays round the
thee, our love - ly Queen, in thrall; Or be the haunt of
sf
sf
cas - tle's moat Is on - ly the warder's ran - dom shot; Put
trai - tors, sold, While Scot - land has hands and hearts so bold; Then
off, put off, and row with speed, For now is the time and the hour of need.
steers - man, steers - man, on with speed, For now is the time and the hour of need.
sf
sf
3. Hark, hark the a - lar - um bell hath rung, The
sf
f

war - der's voice hath trea - son sung! The ech - oes to — the fal - con - et's roar, Chime
sweet - ly to — the dash - ing oar: Let tow'r and hall and bat - tle - ments gleam, We
steer by the light of the ta - per's beam; For Scot - land and Ma - ry on with speed, For
now is the time and the hour — of need.
sf
sf

RED, RED IS THE PATH TO GLORY
('STU MO RÙN)

Old Highland Melody
Accompaniment by HELEN HOPEKIRK

Dr. ROBERT COUPER (1750-1818)

rit.
mf a tempo
Turn _ and _ hear my bod - ing _ cry,
Wae _ was _ me, wi' thee _ to _ part!
Joy of my heart;
rit.
mf
Geor - die, A - gam,
Joy of my heart,
rit.
'Stu mo Rùn!
rit.
mf
pp rit.
f

SAD AM I, AND SORROW-LADEN
(SOIRIDH !)

Written by a young Gael on leaving his native isle

Old Air of the Hebrides
From the "Celtic Lyre"
Accompaniment by HELEN HOPEKIRK

With pathos

VOICE

PIANO

1. Sad am I, and sor - row-lad - en, For the maid I love so well; I a - dore thee, dear - est maid - en, But my thoughts I dare not tell. Why de - ny my heart is rend - ing For the fair one of the lea; Aft - er all my care - ful tend - ing She has now for - sak - en me.

2. Ben of peaks the clouds that sev - er, Oft thy steeps have wear - ied me; Must I leave thy shade for - ev - er? Then fare - well, fare - well to thee! Ev - 'ry cor - rie, crag and hol - low, Heath - 'ry brae and flow - 'ry dell, Now a - wak - en pangs of sor - row, But my thoughts I dare not tell.

p *rit.* *a tempo*

mf
3.Moun-tain bold! thy form sur-pass-es Ev-'ry
p
ben that eye can see; Long may deer fre-quent thy pass-es, Near thee I would ev-er be. Sad am
rit.
a tempo
I and sor-row-lad-en, For the maid I love so well; I a-dore thee, dear-est
maid-en, But my thoughts I dare not tell.
pp rit.

SEE AFAR YON HILL ARDMORE
(THE PRAISE OF ISLAY)
MOLADH NA LANDAIDH

Old Gaelic Verses
Translated by Thomas Pattison (1828-1865)

Ancient Gaelic Air
From the "Celtic Lyre"
Accompaniment by HELEN HOPEKIRK

CHORUS
with enthusiasm
O, my Is-land! O, my Isle! O, my dear, my na-tive soil!
f a tempo
Naught from thee my heart can wile, That's wed with love to Is-lay.
4. Bir-ken branch-es there are gay, Haw-thorns wave their sil-ver'd spray;
5. Ma-vis sings on ha-zel bough, Lin-nets haunt the glen be-low;

Ev - 'ry bough the breez - es sway, A - wak - ens joy in Is - lay.
O, may long their wild notes flow With mel - o - dies in Is - lay.
CHORUS
f
O, my Is - land, O, my Isle, O, my dear, my na - tive soil;
f
sf
sf
Naught from thee my heart can wile, That's wed with love to Is - lay.
f
p

SCOTS, WHA HAE WI' WALLACE BLED

A version of an old air
"Hey, tuttie tattie"
Accompaniment by HELEN HOPEKIRK

ROBERT BURNS (1759-1796)

now's the hour; See the front of
king and law Free - dom's sword will
surp - ers low! Ty - rants fall in
bat - tle lour! See ap - proach proud Ed - ward's power,
strong - ly draw, Free - man stand, or free - man fa',
ev - 'ry foe! Li - ber - ty's in ev - 'ry blow!
Chains an' sla - ver - ie!
Let him fol - low me!
Let us do or die!

SHOULD AULD ACQUAINTANCE BE FORGOT
(AULD LANG SYNE)

Old verses, partly rewritten
by ROBERT BURNS (1759-1796)

Old Tune
Accompaniment by HELEN HOPEKIRK

rall.
auld lang syne, We'll tak' a cup o' kind-ness now, For
rall.
auld lang syne.
f a tempo
p
3. We twa hae run a-bout the braes, And pu'd the gow-ans fine; We've
4. And here's a hand, my trust-y fere, And gi'es a hand o' thine; We'll
rall.
a tempo
wan-der'd mon-y a wear-y foot, Sin' auld lang syne.
tak' a richt gude wil-lie waught For auld lang syne.
For
rall.
a tempo

auld lang syne, my dear, For auld lang syne We'll
tak' a cup o' kind-ness now, For the days o' auld lang syne.
rall.
rall.
a tempo
5. And sure-ly ye'll be
your pint-stoup, And sure-ly I'll be mine, We'll tak' a cup o'

rall.
a tempo
kind - ness yet For the sake o' auld lang syne. For auld lang
rall.
a tempo
syne my dear, For auld lang syne, We'll tak' a cup o'
rall.
rall.
f very quickly
kind - ness yet, For auld lang syne. For auld lang syne, my dear, For
f
auld lang syne, We'll tak' a cup o' kind - ness yet For auld lang syne.
rall.
rall.

SINCE MY LOVED ONE HAS GONE
(MO NIGHEAN CHRUINN, DONN)

From the old Gaelic
Translated by "Fionn" (Henry Whyte)

Old Gaelic Air
From the "Celtic Lyre"
Accompaniment by HELEN HOPEKIRK

love, free-ly roam - ing; Were I now with my
way in Glen Iu - ray; Thou art now far a-
L.H.
cresc.
love, 'Neath the shade of the grove, To hear the coo-ing dove In the
way Sad by night and by day While here I pine al-way, Naught can
rit.
p a tempo
a tempo
gloam - ing.
cure me.
L.H.
p
3. Bear my love to the maid, once so cheer-ful; Bear my love to the
mf

p rit.
maid, whom I'll nev - er up-braid, For now she's low-ly laid, Sad and
p rit.
a tempo
tear - ful. Tis an old carl, I hear, wooed my maid - en, Tis an old carl, I
a tempo
pp
rit.
hear, With his gold and his gear, And now he's left my dear Sor-row-
pp
rit.
lad - en.
L.H.
L.H.
L.H.
a tempo
rit.

SMILE NA SAE SWEET, MY BONNIE BABE
(FINE FLOWERS IN THE VALLEY)

mp
pp
3. She's tak - en out her wee pen - knife, (Fine flow'rs in the
4. She's how - kit a grave by the licht o' the moon, (Fine flow'rs in the
5. As she was go - ing to the church, (Fine flow'rs in the
mp
pp
mp
val - ley) And twin'd the sweet babe o' its life: (And the
val - ley) And there she bur - ied her sweet babe: (And the
val - ley) She saw a wee babe in the porch: (And the
pp
pp
green leaves they grow rare - ly.)
green leaves they grow rare - ly.)
green leaves they grow rare - ly.)
p

mp
pp
6 O my sweet babe, an' thou wert mine, (Fine flow'rs in the
7 O mith - er dear, when I was thine, (Fine flow'rs in the
val - ley) I wad clead thee in the silk sae fine: (And the
val - ley) Ye did na prove to me sae kin': (And the
green leaves they grow rare - ly.)
green leaves they grow rare - ly.)
1.
last time
p

SING THE PRAISES O' MY DEARIE

(THE PEERLESS MAIDEN)

From the Gaelic of "Fionn" (Henry Whyte)
Translated by Malcolm MacFarlane

Old Gaelic Air
From the "Celtic Lyre"
Accompaniment by HELEN HOPEKIRK

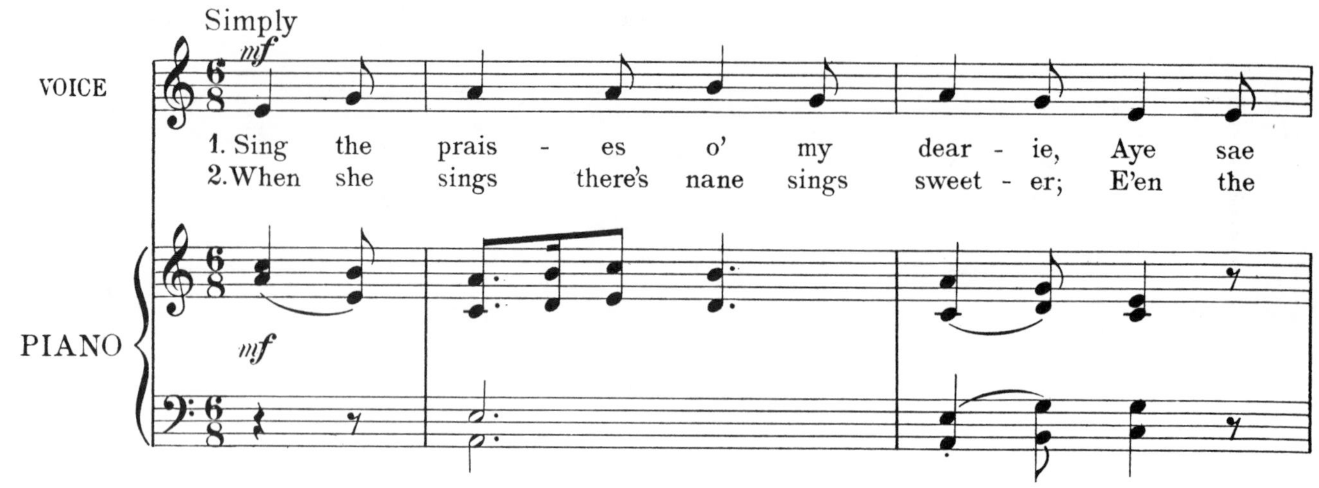

rear'd a - mang the Hie - lans, Land o' crofts and sum - mer
il - ka ane comes near her, And the long - er kenn'd the
shie - lins; How it charms and warms the feel - ins When she
dear - er; North or south there's nane can peer her; And she's
Gael - ic speaks tae me.
a' the warld tae me.
rit.
3.Though a - far frae her I
p

wan - der, On my dear ane still_ I pon - der; Il - ka day but makes me
f
rit.
a tempo
fond - er Love like mine can nev - er die. From the day when first I
rit.
a tempo
met her, My de - sire has been to get her; Come what may I'll ne'er for -
get her, Un - til death shall close my e'e.
pp

THE LAIRD O' COCKPEN

Lady CAROLINA NAIRNE (1766-1845)

Very ancient Scottish Melody
Accompaniment by HELEN HOPEKIRK

mf
3. He mount-ed his mare an' he rade can-ni-lie, An' rapp'd at the yett o'
4. Mistress Jean she was mak-in' the el-der-flow'r wine,"What the deil brings the Laird here at
mf
Cla-vers-ha' Lee. "Gae tell mis-tress Jean to come speed-i-ly ben, She's
sic a like time?" She put off her a-pron, and on her silk gown, Her
want-ed to speak wi' the Laird o' Cock-pen."
mutch wi' red rib-bons, an' gae'd a-wa' doon.
p

mf
5. An' when she came ben she bob-bit fu' low, And what was his er-rand he
6. Dumb-found-ed was he, but nae sigh did he gie; He mount-ed his mare an' he
mf
soon let her know; A-maz'd was the Laird, when the la-dy said "Na;" An'
rode can-ni-lie; An' af-ten he thocht, as he gae'd thro' the glen, "She was
rit.
rit.
a tempo
wi' a laigh curt-sie she turn-ed a-wa'.
daft to re-fuse the Laird o' Cock-pen."
a tempo
f

THE CAMPBELLS ARE COMIN'

Verses written about 1715,
at the period of the Scottish Rebellion

Melody of an old Scottish Dance
Accompaniment by HELEN HOPEKIRK

lay, I lay, I look - ed down to bon - nie, Loch Lev - en, And
guns to roar Wi' sound o' trump - et pipe and drum, The
truth to show; Wi' ban - ners rat - tling in the wind, The
saw three bon - nie perch - es play.
Campbells are com - in', O - ho, O - ho!
Campbells are com - in', O - ho, O - ho!
The Campbells are com - in', O - ho, O - ho! The
Campbells are com - in', O - ho, O - ho! The Campbells are com - in', to bon - nie Loch Leven; The
Campbells are com - in', O - ho, O - ho!
ff
sf

THE DE'IL CAM' FIDDLIN' THRO' THE TOUN

(THE DE'IL'S AWA' WI' THE EXCISEMAN)

ROBERT BURNS (1759-1796)

Melody probably Old English
Accompaniment by HELEN HOPEKIRK

il - ka auld wife_ cried "Auld Ma - houn,_ We wish you luck o' the prize, man!"
mon - y braw thanks to the muck - le black De'il,_ That's danc'd a - wa' wi' th' Ex - cise - man!" The
aye the best dance_ e'er came to our land Was the De'il's a - wa' wi' th' Ex - cise - man!"
faster
De'il's a - wa',_ the De'il's a - wa' He's danc'd a - wa' wi' th' Ex - cise - man! O
mon - y braw thanks to the muck - le black De'il, That's danc'd a - wa' wi' th' Ex - cise - man!
dim.
dim. rit.
pp

THE NEWS FRAE MOIDART CAM' YESTREEN
(WHA'LL BE KING BUT CHARLIE?)

Lady CAROLINA NAIRNE (1766-1845)

Melody common in Ireland and Scotland
Accompaniment by HELEN HOPEKIRK

a tempo
ear - ly, A - round him cling wi' a' your kin, For wha'll be King _ but
rit.
a tempo
f
Char - lie? Come through the heath - er, a - round him gath - er, Come Ronald, come Donald, come
f
f
sf
rit.
a tempo
rit.
a tempo
a' _ the - gith - er, And crown your right - fu', law - fu' King! For wha'll be King, but
rit.
a tempo
rit.
a tempo
Char - lie?
sf

f
3. The Low-lands a', baith great and sma', Wi' mon-y a lord and laird, Hae' de-
4. Then here's a health to Char-lie's cause, An' be it com-plete an' ear-ly, His
clar'd for Sco-tia's king and law, And spier ye wha, but Char-lie!
ver-y name our heart's bluid warms; To arms for Roy-al Char-lie!
Come
through the heath-er, a-round him gath-er, Ye're a' the wel-com-er ear-ly. A-
round him cling wi' a' your kin, For wha'll be King but Char-lie? Come
rit.
a tempo
sf

rit.
through the heath-er, a-round him gath-er, Come Ronald, come Donald, come a'— the gith-er, And
f
f
sf
rit.
a tempo
rit.
a tempo
crown your right - fu', law - fu' King! For wha'll be king— but Char - lie?
a tempo
rit.
a tempo
sf
After 3rd verse
f
After last verse
f
sf

THE WINTER IT IS PAST

Verses from "Johnson's Museum"

Melody from "Johnson's Museum"
Accompaniment by HELEN HOPEKIRK

3. My love is like the sun that in the sky doth run, Forever as constant and true; But his is like the moon that wanders up and down, And ev-'ry month it is new.
4. All you that are in love, and cannot it remove, I pity the pains you endure, For experience makes me know your hearts are full of woe, A woe that no mortal can cure.
a tempo
p
rit.
a tempo
p
rit.

THERE GROWS A BONNIE BRIER-BUSH

Air sent by Burns
to "Johnson's Museum"
Accompaniment by HELEN HOPEKIRK (*

Lady CAROLINA NAIRNE (1766-1845)

2. He's com-in' frae the north that's to fan-cy_ me; He's_
com-in' frae the north that's to fan-cy_ me; A feath-er in his bon-net, a
rib-bon at his knee, He's a_ bon-nie Hie-land lad-die, and
you'll na be he!
cresc.
rit.
a tempo
D.S. al Fine (for 3rd Verse)
L.H.

THREE SCORE O' NOBLES RADE UP THE KING'S HA'
(GLENOGIE)

a tempo
f
4. Then to Glen-fel-dy's, but sma' mirth was there, An' bonnie Jean's mith-er was tear-in' her hair, "Ye're welcome, Glen-o-gie, ye're wel-come!" quo' she, "Ye're wel-come, Glen-o-gie, your Jean-ie to see."
5. Pale and wan was she when Glen-o-gie gae'd ben, But ros-y red grew she when-e'er he sat doun; She turn-ed a-wa' wi' a smile in her e'e, "O dinna fear, mith-er, I'll may-be no dee!"
rit.
after 4th verse
after last verse
p
f

THE MOON HAD CLIMBED THE HIGHEST HILL

(MARY'S DREAM)

ALEXANDER LOWE
(of Galloway)

From "Johnson's Museum"
Accompaniment by HELEN HOPEKIRK

When Mary laid her down to sleep Her thoughts on Sandy far at sea When soft and low a voice was heard say, "Mary, weep no more for me."
Ah, Mary dear, cold is my clay; It lies beneath a stormy sea, Far, far from thee, I sleep in death, So, "Mary, weep no more for me."
pp
3. O maiden dear, thyself prepare, We soon shall meet up-

on that shore Where love is freed from doubt and care, And
pp
pp
thou and I shall part no more. Loud crow'd the cock, the
mf
shad-ow fled, No more of San-dy could she see, But soft the pass-ing
pp
pp
spir-it said "Sweet Ma-ry, weep no more for me."
rit.
pp
rit.
pp

TURN YE TO ME

JOHN WILSON (*Christopher North*) 1785-1854

Melody from "Songs of the North"
Accompaniment by HELEN HOPEKIRK

rit.
a tempo
drear - i - ly, Ho - ro Mhai - ri dhu, turn ye to me.
mf
Cold is the
rit.
a tempo
mf
storm-wind that ruf-fles his breast, But warm are the down - y plumes
mp
rit.
expressively
lin - ing his nest. Cold blows the storm there, soft falls the
a tempo
pp
rit.
snow there, Ho - ro Mhai - ri dhu, turn ye to me.
a tempo
rit.

mf
The
a tempo
waves are danc - ing mer - ri - ly, mer - ri - ly,
p
Ho - ro Mhai - ri dhu, turn ye — to me. The sea-birds are
p
rit.
a tempo
wail - ing wear - i - ly, wear - i - ly, Ho - ro Mhai - ri dhu,
rit.
a tempo

p
turn ye — to me.
Hushed by thy moan-ing, lone bird of the
p
cresc.
sea, Thy home on the rocks is a shel-ter to thee. Thy
cresc.
pp
rit.
a tempo
home is the an-gry wave, mine but the lone-ly grave, Ho-ro
pp
rit.
a tempo
rit.
Mhai-ri dhu, turn ye — to me.
Ped.
Ped.

THY CHEEK IS O' THE ROSE'S HUE

Melody of the 18th Century
Accompaniment by HELEN HOPEKIRK

RICHARD GALL (1776-1801)

i - vo - ry, O, sweet's the twin - kle_ o' thine e'e Nae_
owre the lee, And round a - bout the_ thorn - y tree, Or_
rit.
joy, nae pleas - ure_ blinks on me, My on - ly jo_ and_ dear - ie, O.
pu' the wild - flow'rs a' for thee, My on - ly jo_ and_ dear - ie, O.
p a tempo
mp
2. The bird - ie sings up - on the thorn, It
4. I hae a wish I_ can - na tine, 'Mang
pp
cresc.
sang o' joy_ fu'_ cheer - ie, O, Re - joi - cing in_ the_
a' the cares_ that_ grieve me, O, A wish that thou_ wert_
8

sim - mer morn, Nae care to mak' it eer - ie, O. Ah!
ev - er mine, And nev - er mair to leave thee O. Then
lit - tle kens the sang - ster sweet, Aught o' the cares I
I wad dawt thee night and day, Nae ith - er warld - ly
cresc.
rit.
p
hae to meet, That gars my rest - less bos - om beat, My
care I'd hae, Till life's warm stream for - gat to play, My
a tempo
on - ly jo and dear - ie, O.
on - ly jo and dear - ie, O.
pp

WHY WEEP YE BY THE TIDE, LADYE?
(JOCK O' HAZELDEAN)

Sir WALTER SCOTT (1771-1832)

Melody of the 17th Century
Accompaniment by HELEN HOPEKIRK

p
ye sall be his bride, la-dye, Sae come-ly to be seen!" But
step is first in peace-fu' ha', His sword in bat-tle keen!" But
you the fore-most o' them a', Shall ride our for-est queen!" But
p
rit.
a tempo
aye she loot the tears down fa' For Jock o' Ha-zel-dean.
aye she loot the tears down fa' For Jock o' Ha-zel-dean.
aye she loot the tears down fa' For Jock o' Ha-zel-dean.
rit.
a tempo
mf
4. The

mf
kirk was deck'd at morning tide, The tapers glim-mer'd fair; The
priest and bride-groom wait the bride, And dame and knight were there;
p
They sought her baith by bow'r and ha', The
pp rit.
la-dye was not seen!
a tempo
f
She's o'er the border and a-wa' Wi' Jock o' Ha-zel-dean!
f a tempo
ff
p
cresc.
f

WINSOME MARY
(MAIRI LAGHACH)

From the Gaelic of J. Macdonald
Translated by Evan McColl

From the "Celtic Lyre"
Accompaniment by HELEN HOPEKIRK

f
p
mf
3.What al-though all Al-binn And its wealth were mine, How, with-out thee,dar-ling,
4.What a wealth of tress-es Ma-ry dear can show! Crown of lus-tre rar-er
mf
Could I fail to pine? As my bride to kiss thee I would prize far more
Ne'er graced maid-en brow! 'Tis but lit-tle dress-ing Need those tress-es rare
p
p
Than the all of treas-ure Eu-rope has in store.
Fall-ing fond-ly, proud-ly O'er her shoul-ders fair.
L.H.
p

pp
rit.
mf
5. No mere mu-sic art-born e'er our pleas-ure crowned, Mu-sic far more cheer-ing
a tempo
Na-ture for us found. Larks in air, and thrush-es On each flow-'ring thorn,
p
cresc.
f
And the cuck-oo hail-ing Sum-mer's gay re-turn!
L.H.
pp
rit.

WHAR' HA'E YE BEEN A' THE DAY
(MY BOY TAMMY)

Court - in' o' this young thing Just come frae her mammie.
Herd - ing ae wee lamb an' yowe For her puir — mammie.
pree'd it aft as ye may trow! She said she'd tell her mammie.

rit. *rit.* *pp*

4. I held her to my beat - in' heart, My young my smil - ing lammie; I
5. Has she been to the kirk wi' thee, My — boy — Tammy? Has

pp

held her to my beat - in' heart, My young, my smil - ing lammie. I hae a house, it cost me dear, I've
she been to the kirk wi' thee, My — boy — Tammy? O, she's been to the kirk wi' me,

rit. *a tempo*

wealth o' plen-ish-ing an' gear, Ye'se get it a', wer't ten times mair, Gin ye will leave your mammie.
An' the tear was in her e'e, For O! she's but a young — thing, Just come frae her mammie!

rit.

WHAT'S THIS DULL TOWN TO ME?
(ROBIN ADAIR)

Old Celtic Air, common to Scotland and Ireland
Accompaniment by HELEN HOPEKIRK

cresc. agitato
Where's all the joy and mirth Made this town heav'n on earth? O they're all fled wi' thee, Rob - in A - dair.
What, when the play was o'er, What made my heart so sore? O, it was part - ing with Rob - in A - dair.
Yet he I lov'd so well, Still in my heart shall dwell; Oh, I can ne'er for - get Rob - in A - dair.
cresc.
f
p
rit.
1st and 2nd time
Last time
pp
L.H.
L.H.

WHERE SLEEPEST THOU, MY DEARIE?

Translated from the Gaelic
by "Fionn" (Henry Whyte)

Melody from the "Celtic Lyre"
Accompaniment by HELEN HOPEKIRK

a tempo
mf
near thee. My ship is float - ing on the tide, And pros - per - ous winds are
dear - ie. My sails are set; blow, breez - es, blow! All thoughts of dan - ger
mf a tempo
cresc.
blow - ing; If thou wert on - ly by my side, My
scorn - ing; Where dwells my love I'll quick - ly go And
cresc.
tears would not be flow - ing.
wed her in the morn - ing.
pp

WILL YE GANG TO THE HIELANDS, LEEZIE LINDSAY?

Old Scottish Ballad

Air from "Johnson's Museum"
Accompaniment by HELEN HOPEKIRK

be?
gree."
2. "To
4. She has
gang to the Hie-lands wi' you, sir,
kilt - ed her coats o' green sa - tin,
I din - na ken
She has kilt - ed them
how that may be;
up to her knee;
For I ken na the land that you
And she's off wi' Lord Ron - ald Mac -
live in,
Don-ald,
Nor ken I the lad I'm gaun wi'."
His bride and his dar - ling to be.

WITH THE LOORGEEN O HEE
(LEIS AN LURGAINN)

Translated from Sinclair's "Oranaiche"
by Malcolm MacFarlane of Paisley

Old Boat song of the West Coast of Scotland
From the "Celtic Lyre"
Accompaniment by HELEN HOPEKIRK

f
On the o - cean, o hee, Waves in mo - tion, O
A - ros pass - ing, o hee, Twas ha - rass - ing, O
Bil - lows lash - ing, o hee, Wa - ters crash - ing, O
ho, Nought but clouds could we see O'er the blue sea be - low.
ho, The strong bil - lows to see High as mast - head to flow.
ho, With - out blench - ing we see There be stout hearts on board.
sf
dim.

YE BANKS AND BRAES O' BONNIE DOON

ROBERT BURNS (1759-1796)

Air composed by JAMES MILLER
(Published in 1788)
Accompaniment by HELEN HOPEKIRK

rit.
a tempo
cresc.
I___ sae wear - y, fu'___ o' care! Thou'll break my heart, thou
fond - ly sae___ did I___ o' mine! Wi' light - some heart I
war - bling bird,___ That wan - tons through the flow' - ring thorn; Thou
pu'd a rose,___ Fu' sweet___ up - on___ its thorn - y tree; But
p
minds me o'___ de - part - ed joys,___ De - part - ed, nev - er to___ re-turn!
my fause lov - er stole my rose,___ But ah! he left the thorn wi' me!
rit.

YOUNG JAMIE LO'ED ME WEEL

(AULD ROBIN GRAY)

Air by WILLIAM LEEVES
(First Published in 1812)
Accompaniment by HELEN HOPEKIRK

Lady ANNE LINDSAY (1750-1825)

agitato
crown and the pound were baith for me. He had-na been a-wa' a
"Jen-ny, for their sakes, O mar-ry me." My heart it said nay, for I
week but on-ly twa, When my fa-ther brak his arm, and the
look'd for Ja-mie back, But the wind it blew high and the
p
cow was stown a-wa'; My mith-er she fell sick, and
ship it was a wrack. The ship it was a wrack, why
p
rit.
a tempo
rit.
Ja-mie at the sea, And auld Rob-in Gray cam' a-court-in' me.
did-na Ja-mie dee? And why do I live to say, wae's me!
rit.
a tempo

a tempo
3. My fa - ther urged me sair, my
4. O sair did we greet, and
p
a tempo
mith - er did - na speak But look'd in my face till my
meik - le did we say, We took but ae kiss and we
heart was like to break; So they gi'ed him my hand, my
tore our - selves a - way; I wish I were deid, but
rit.
a tempo
heart it was at sea, And auld Rob - in Gray is a
I'm no like to dee; Oh! why do I live to
rit.
a tempo

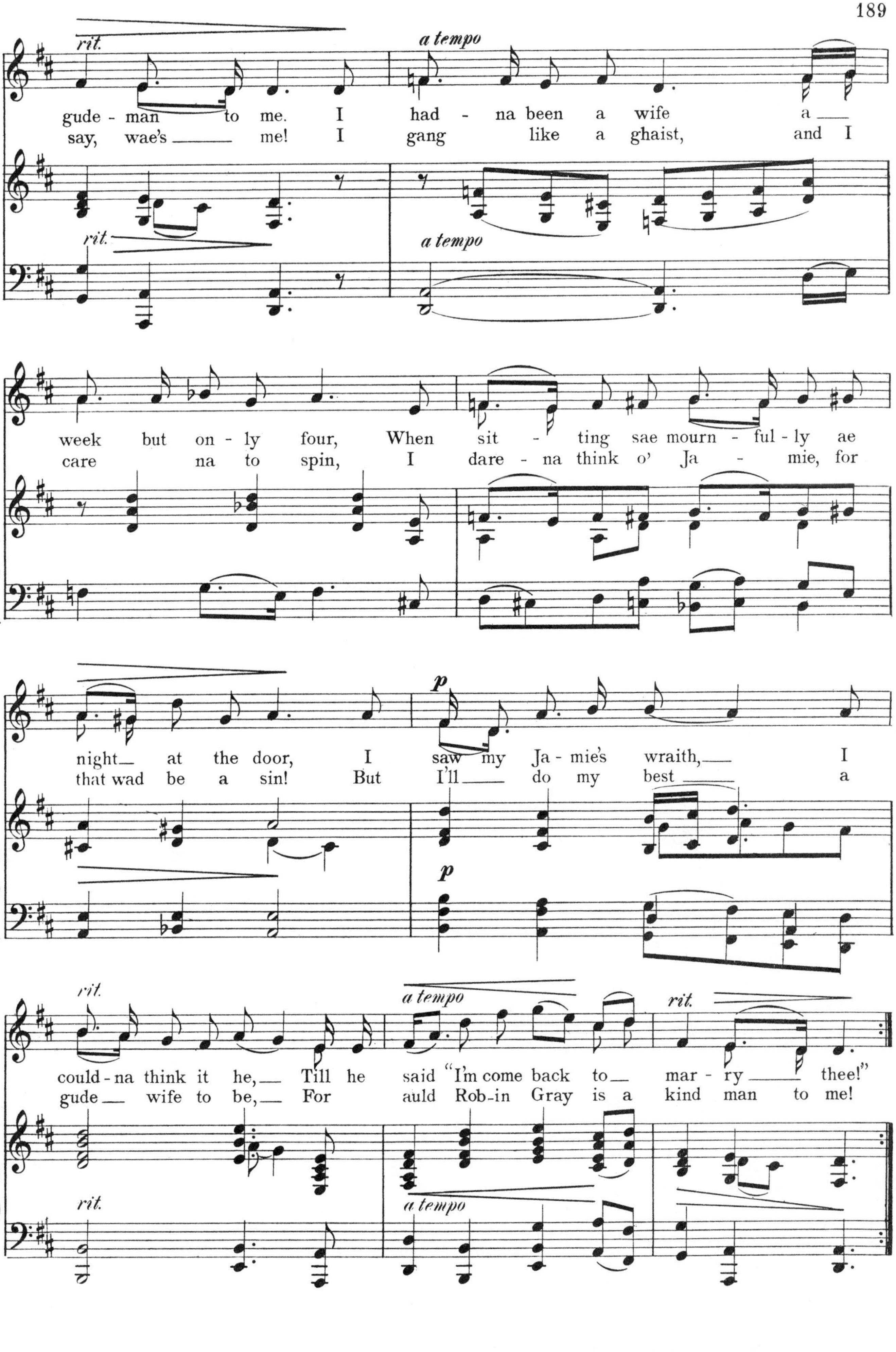
rit.
a tempo
gude - man to me. I had - na been a wife a
say, wae's me! I gang like a ghaist, and I
rit.
a tempo
week but on - ly four, When sit - ting sae mourn - ful - ly ae
care na to spin, I dare - na think o' Ja - mie, for
p
night at the door, I saw my Ja - mie's wraith, I
that wad be a sin! But I'll do my best a
p
rit.
a tempo
rit.
could - na think it he, Till he said "I'm come back to mar - ry thee!"
gude wife to be, For auld Rob-in Gray is a kind man to me!
rit.
a tempo

Dover Popular Songbooks

"FOR ME AND MY GAL" AND OTHER FAVORITE SONG HITS, 1915–1917, David A. Jasen (ed.). 31 great hits: Pretty Baby, MacNamara's Band, Over There, Old Grey Mare, Beale Street, M-O-T-H-E-R, more, with original sheet music covers, complete vocal and piano. 144pp. 9 × 12. 28127-2 Pa. **$9.95**

POPULAR IRISH SONGS, Florence Leniston (ed.). 37 all-time favorites with vocal and piano arrangements: "My Wild Irish Rose," "Irish Eyes are Smiling," "Last Rose of Summer," "Danny Boy," many more. 160pp. 26755-5 Pa. **$9.95**

FAVORITE SONGS OF THE NINETIES, edited by Robert Fremont. 88 favorites: "Ta-Ra-Ra-Boom-De-Aye," "The Band Played on," "Bird in a Gilded Cage," etc. 401pp. 9 × 12. 21536-9 Pa. **$15.95**

POPULAR SONGS OF NINETEENTH-CENTURY AMERICA, edited by Richard Jackson. 64 most important songs: "Old Oaken Bucket," "Arkansas Traveler," "Yellow Rose of Texas," etc. 290pp. 9 × 12. 23270-0 Pa. **$12.95**

SONG HITS FROM THE TURN OF THE CENTURY, edited by Paul Charosh, Robert A. Fremont. 62 bit hits: "Silver Heels," "My Sweetheart's the Man in the Moon," etc. 296pp. 9 × 12. (Except British Commonwealth [but may be sold in Canada]) 23158-5 Pa. **$8.95**

ALEXANDER'S RAGTIME BAND AND OTHER FAVORITE SONG HITS, 1901–1911, edited by David A. Jasen. Fifty vintage popular songs America still sings, reprinted in their entirety from the original editions. Introduction. 224pp. 9 × 12. (Available in U.S. only) 25331-7 Pa. **$11.95**

"PEG O' MY HEART" AND OTHER FAVORITE SONG HITS, 1912 & 1913, edited by Stanley Appelbaum. 36 songs by Berlin, Herbert, Handy and others, with complete lyrics, full piano arrangements and original sheet music covers in black and white. 176pp. 9 × 12. 25998-6 Pa. **$12.95**

SONGS OF THE CIVIL WAR, Irwin Silber (ed.). Piano, vocal, guitar chords for 125 songs including *Battle Cry of Freedom, Marching Through Georgia, Dixie, Oh, I'm a Good Old Rebel, The Drummer Boy of Shiloh,* many more. 400pp. 8⅜ × 11. 28438-7 Pa. **$14.95**

AMERICAN BALLADS AND FOLK SONGS, John A. Lomax and Alan Lomax. Over 200 songs, music and lyrics: *Frankie and Albert, John Henry, Frog Went a-Courtin', Down in the Valley, Skip to My Lou,"* other favorites. Notes on each song. 672pp. 5⅜ × 8½. 28276-7 Pa. **$12.95**

"TAKE ME OUT TO THE BALL GAME" AND OTHER FAVORITE SONG HITS, 1906–1908, edited by Lester Levy. 23 favorite songs from the turn-of-the-century with lyrics and original sheet music covers: "Cuddle Up a Little Closer, Lovey Mine," "Harrigan," "Shine on, Harvest Moon," "School Days," other hits. 128pp. 9 × 12. 24662-0 Pa. **$7.95**

THE AMERICAN SONG TREASURY: 100 Favorites, edited by Theodore Raph. Complete piano arrangements, guitar chords and lyrics for 100 best-loved tunes, "Buffalo Gals," "Oh, Suzanna," "Clementine," "Camptown Races," and much more. 416pp. 8⅛ × 11. 25222-1 Pa. **$14.95**

"THE ST. LOUIS BLUES" AND OTHER SONG HITS OF 1914, edited by Sandy Marrone. Full vocal and piano for "By the Beautiful Sea," "Play a Simple Melody," "They Didn't Believe Me," 21 songs in all. 112pp. 9 × 12. **26383-5 Pa. $7.95**

STEPHEN FOSTER SONG BOOK, Stephen Foster. 40 favorites: "Beautiful Dreamer," "Camptown Races," "Jeanie with the Light Brown Hair," "My Old Kentucky Home," etc. 224pp. 9 × 12. 23048-1 Pa. **$8.95**

ONE HUNDRED ENGLISH FOLKSONGS, edited by Cecil J. Sharp. Border ballads, folksongs, collected from all over Great Britain. "Lord Bateman," "Henry Martin," "The Green Wedding," many others. Piano. 235pp. 9 × 12. 23192-5 Pa. **$13.95**

THE CIVIL WAR SONGBOOK, edited by Richard Crawford. 37 songs: "Battle Hymn of the Republic," "Drummer Boy of Shiloh," "Dixie," 33 more. 157pp. 9 × 12. 23422-3 Pa. **$8.95**

SONGS OF WORK AND PROTEST, Edith Fowke, Joe Glazer. 100 important songs: "Union Maid," "Joe Hill," "We Shall Not Be Moved," many more. 210pp. 7⅞ × 10¼. 22899-1 Pa. **$10.95**

A RUSSIAN SONG BOOK, edited by Rose N. Rubin and Michael Stillman. 25 traditional folk songs, plus 19 popular songs by twentieth-century composers. Full piano arrangements, guitar chords. Lyrics in original Cyrillic, transliteration and English translation. With discography. 112pp. 9 × 12. 26118-2 Pa. **$8.95**

FAVORITE CHRISTMAS CAROLS, selected and arranged by Charles J. F. Cofone. Title, music, first verse and refrain of 34 traditional carols in handsome calligraphy; also subsequent verses and other information in type. 79pp. 8⅜ × 11. 20445-6 Pa. **$4.95**

SEVENTY SCOTTISH SONGS, Helen Hopekirk (ed.). Complete piano and vocals for classics of Scottish song: *Flow Gently, Sweet Afton, Comin' thro' the Rye (Gin a Body Meet a Body), The Campbells are Comin', Robin Adair,* many more. 208pp. 8⅜ × 11. 27029-7 Pa. **$10.95**